ACKNOWLEDGMENTS

As I reach the end of yet another academic milestone, I am struck by the

unwavering support I have received from those around me. The title page of this work

may bear only one name, but dozens of people behind the scenes deserve credit for

helping me complete what has been the most difficult production of my life to date.

First and foremost, I must thank my adviser, Dr. Michael Weigold, for the

guidance, support, and motivation he has generously given me during the past three years.

I was constantly amazed of the faith he had in me throughout the entire process,

especially the times when I had very little faith in myself. In addition to helping me see

the value of a solid theoretical base, Dr. Weigold deserves credit for any strength the

reader might find in this study. Any errors or omissions, of course, are my own.

The other members of my supervisory committee each deserve special thanks for

their contributions: Dr. Mary Ann Ferguson, for teaching me the foundation of

experimental design and for the continuous confidence she has shown in me; Dr. Marilyn

Roberts, for sharing her vast knowledge of political advertising and for the faith she

showed in joining my committee very late in the game; Dr. Alan Sawyer, for helping me

finally understand the intricacies of research methods and for making my defense an

enjoyable learning experience; and Dr. John Wright, for his valuable insights into the

research process and for his direction and assistance from the first day I entered the Ph.D.

program. I consider myself fortunate to have worked with this group of outstanding scholars and genuinely kind individuals.

Many others at the College of Journalism and Communications helped me throughout the process. Thanks to fellow doctoral student James Karrh for allowing me to use his class for the experiment and to senior Cheryl Urbas, my unofficial research assistant, for her help collecting and entering the data. Doris Lowenstein and Pat Wickham in the dean's office were instrumental in helping with the logistics of the experiment, and Jody Hedge in the graduate division deserves much more than thanks for leading me through the administrative hoops while my mind was occupied elsewhere.

I owe my sanity to those outside the halls of academe who were there throughout the process. My husband, Richard LeComte--my best friend, champion, and editor--has made many sacrifices both professionally and personally so that I could peruse my graduate degrees. I owe him more than I can ever repay. My daughter, Rachel LeComte, has inspired me from the first second I saw her and brings me joy daily. My temporary hometown of Palatka, Florida, was filled with people cheering me on. Special thanks to the two Mistys--Higgins and Cannon--for their friendship and help with Rachel. My sister, Vicki Greer, provided encouragement and much-needed levity long distance.

Finally, I must thank my parents, Donald and Dixie Greer, for their love and support during the past 30 years. My mother taught me from an early age that I could have it all--a family and career--with some delicate balancing. My father gave me a love of learning, intense stubbornness, and a drive for perfection that has allowed me to accomplish my goals. This dissertation is dedicated to them.

iii

TABLE OF CONTENTS

page

ACKNOWLEDGMENTS ii

ABSTRACT vi

CHAPTERS

   I. INTRODUCTION. 1

      Overview 1
      Political Campaigns: A Brief Historical Perspective 3
      Current Issues in Political Advertising 6
      The Turning Point: 1988 . . . .
      9
      Journalist Response: The Ad Cops are Deputized 11
      The Problem with Adwatches 17
      Problem Definition 19

   II. LITERATURE REVIEW 22

      Adwatch Research 22
      Persuasion Research: A Brief History 36
      The Elaboration Likelihood Model of Persuasion 38
      Need for Cognition 55
      Hypotheses 59

   III. METHOD 66

      An Overview 66
      Independent Variables 73
      Dependent Variables 87
      Path for Analysis 90

IV. RESULTS 92

    Descriptive Analysis 92
    The Scales 95
    Assumptions 99
    Manipulation Checks 101
    Tests of Hypotheses 106
    Research Questions 115

V. DISCUSSION 119

    Summary of Results 120
    Post-Hoc Analysis 122
    Problems and Limitations 130
    Implications 132
    Directions for Future Study 139

APPENDICES

  A   INFORMED CONSENT FORM 142
  B   BIOGRAPHICAL SKETCHES OF THE CANDIDATES 143
  C   TEXT OF THE COMMERCIAL USED AS STIMULUS 144
  D   HIGH AND LOW-QUALITY ADWATCHES USED AS STIMULUS . 145
  E   THE FLORIDA TIMES-UNION ADWATCH 147
  F   QUESTIONNAIRE 148

REFERENCES 157

BIOGRAPHICAL SKETCH 170

Abstract of Dissertation Presented to the Graduate School
of the University Of Florida in Partial Fulfillment of the
Requirements for the Degree of Doctor of Philosophy

UNLEASHING THE WATCHDOGS ON POLITICAL ADVERTISING:
THE INFLUENCE OF NEED FOR COGNITION,
ARGUMENT QUALITY, AND SOURCE CREDIBILITY
ON NEWSPAPER ADWATCH EFFECTIVENESS

By

Jennifer D. Greer
August 1996

Chairman: Michael F. Weigold
Major Department: Journalism: Journalism and Communications

In response to a perceived rash of "false" and "misleading" advertising in the

1988 presidential race, news organizations started producing "adwatches" during

campaigns. Journalists designed adwatches to police political advertising, especially ads

containing misleading claims or images, and to help voters make better informed choices.

This dissertation adds to a small but growing body of adwatch research that

examines the effects of adwatch exposure on voters' attitudes toward commercials and

their sponsoring candidates. Applying the Elaboration Likelihood Model (ELM) of

persuasion, this research examines whether adwatches affect attitudes in general and

under what conditions and with which individuals effects are most likely to occur. An

experimental design was used to test three independent variables: Need for cognition;

argument quality, and source credibility. It was predicted that attitudes held by subjects high in the need for cognition toward a commercial and its sponsoring candidate would be influenced only by high-quality adwatches. In contrast, low-need-for-cognition subjects would be influenced only by highly credible adwatch sources.

The research replicated past findings that adwatch exposure is linked to more critical evaluations of an advertisement. Tests suggested by the individual differences approach of the ELM found that adwatch exposure only resulted in lower evaluations of the advertisement among high-need-for-cognition voters. Low-need-for-cognition subjects appeared unaffected. Further, only those high-need-for-cognition subjects who read a high-quality adwatch appeared to be influenced by the adwatch.

While attitudes about the ad were affected, candidate evaluation was not, possibly because the sponsoring candidate did not appear in the ad. In addition, manipulating source credibility had no effect on any of the subjects, regardless of need for cognition, possibly because past research has shown that source credibility is not a factor that determines influence of negative communications.

The results suggest that adwatches can affect attitudes of some voters--those classified as high in the need for cognition--and under some circumstances, namely when adwatch argument quality is high. However, these subjects were less likely to say they would read adwatch features during an election. If these findings are replicated in other settings, journalists might rethink the utility and value of adwatches.

CHAPTER I
INTRODUCTION

Overview

For newspaper wire editors, the stories carried over the political wires on June 6, 1996, provided a vivid example of the recent revolution that had transformed campaign coverage in the United States. In an eight-hour block on that date, the Associated Press moved an article about Sen. Bob Dole's speech in Nashville, a brief article about a planned campaign appearance by President Bill Clinton in San Francisco, and a few other stories about statewide races. The mere smattering of stories about campaign appearances and strategy moved on that day was hardly surprising, given that the general election was still five months away. After all, the political parties had not even formally nominated the two candidates. In this regard, the political news wire virtually mirrored the AP's political coverage during the same month in 1988.

But wire editors were faced with a whole new category of campaign stories to chose from in the 1996 election that was non-existent eight years prior. While the AP moved only two "traditional" campaign stories about the presidential race on June 6, 1996, the wire carried three major articles on political advertising--a story about Dole's advertising strategy, an "adwatch" of a Dole commercial, and an "adwatch" of a commercial aired in the Virginia Senate primary. The day's political news selection was typical of the AP's news coverage in the 1996 race. During the early Republican primaries, when several major candidates were vying for the party's nomination, the

Associated Press' political wire routinely carried two or more adwatches a day.[1]

The Associated Press political coverage of the 1996 races represents a new era in

political reporting that began after the 1988 presidential election. The term "adwatch"

was only been coined in 1990. But within six years, news coverage of political

advertising--including adwatches--were almost on equal ground with "traditional"

campaign news, such as coverage of debates, speeches, and the like. Adwatches are a

device used by all types of news organizations to examine claims made in political

advertising. Typically, adwatches are aimed at exposing "false" or "misleading"

statements or visuals in campaign commercials that, in principle, can deceive voters

exposed to them. The journalistic rationale behind producing adwatches is that voters,

trying to sort through competing claims in a sea of deceptive campaign commercials, can

turn to a credible independent voice--the news media--for help in deciding what is true

and what is not true.

Adwatches and other types of political advertising coverage by the news media

became so prominent in the 1990s that political communication researchers took notice.

By the mid 1990s, a handful of studies systematically examining adwatches began to

emerge. Content analyses reviewed the scope and nature of reporting on political

commercials. Surveys tracked the public's perception of adwatches and news coverage

of political advertising. Experiments examined what effects, if any, the new form of

[1] Information about the Associated Press' political wire coverage on June 6, 1996, was collected by the researcher, who at the time worked as managing editor of Sun.ONE, a commercial on-line newspaper produced by the University of Florida's College of Journalism and Communications and The Gainesville Sun.

coverage had on its intended audience, the voters. While adwatch research to date has begun to gauge the nature and impact of this new form of political communication, many questions remain unanswered. For example, what role do adwatches play in local races? How does the quality of the information contained in adwatches affect the impact of the critiques? How does credibility of the source producing adwatches affect the influence of adwatches on voter attitudes toward political commercials and their sponsoring candidates? Most importantly, how do individual differences in voters receiving adwatch information affect the impact of adwatches on the public? This study seeks to break ground in the emerging area of adwatch research by examining these questions.

To place this research in perspective, this chapter provides a brief history of political campaigns and the use of advertising as a component in modern campaigns. Next, the key role played by political advertising in the 1988 election is detailed, followed by a look at the journalistic response to those campaign ads. The birth of adwatches and the emergence of a debate about their journalistic appropriateness are then discussed. The chapter ends with a definition of the problem examined by this study.

Political Campaigns: A Brief Historical Perspective

Agranoff (1980) defined political campaigns as "a coordinated effort to achieve the objective of winning an election through the mobilization of human, social, material and environmental resources" (quoted in Meadow, 1989, p. 253). Meadow (1989) argues that campaigns are designed to reach the target audience--voters--at cognitive, affective, and behavioral levels:

> At the cognitive level, a candidate and his or her positions
> must become known to the voters. At the affective level,

4

the candidate must be seen positively and liked, respected,
or admired by the voter. At the behavioral level, the voter
must want to demonstrate support for the candidate by
engaging in a specific behavior--voting (p. 260).

Mass communication, advertising in particular, has increasingly become the key to

reaching voters on these three levels. Trent and Friedenberg (1983) argue that while

economic, sociological, psychological, and historical factors are essential parts of the

electoral process, communication is the core of modern political campaigns. "It is

communication that occupies the area between the goals or aspirations of the candidate

and the behavior of the electorate . . . Hence, communication is the means by which the

campaign begins, proceeds, and concludes" (Trent & Friedenberg, p. 16).

Mass communication-centered modern political campaigns are markedly different

from those envisioned by the nation's founding fathers, who designed a system of

selecting political leaders that bypassed the vast majority of U.S. citizens. A few elites

were supposed to gather in private, analyze the qualifications of men and deliberate on

who might make the best president. Alexander Hamilton argued in The Federalist, No.

68 that the choice of a president would rest on candidates' "requisite qualifications," not

on their "talents for low intrigue and the little arts of popularity" (quoted in Patterson,

1993, p. 38).

After George Washington's election, this ideal quickly evaporated, and candidates

started running on the "little arts of popularity." Pamphlets and rallies touting the virtues

of one candidate while vilifying the opposition marked the second presidential race

(Jamieson, 1992b). Still, in 1790 only white men who owned land could vote. But in

1828, the number of participating voters tripled, and for the first time a mass audience of voters cast ballots for electors committed to particular candidates (Jamieson, 1992b).

Throughout the following 150 years, the enfranchised electorate grew even more to

encompass virtually all U.S. citizens over age 18. With every expansion in the electorate,

politicians sought new ways to reach this increasing number of voters. First came

handbills, posters and newspapers carrying messages about candidates. In the early 20th

century, radio gave candidates the first mass medium to reach potential supporters

(Gronbeck, 1992). The first radio spot commercial appeared in 1936 to support Alf

Landon's doomed presidential bid (Mickelson, 1989).

Within a few decades, television, which has the reach of radio plus a visual

element, became the medium of choice for candidates to reach a diversified audience.

Candidates began using television for campaign advertising almost as soon at the medium

became available. On October 5, 1948, Harry Truman became the first presidential

candidate to buy television time (for a speech), and he may have been the first candidate

to air a televised spot ad (see Jamieson, 1992b, note p. 34). That same year, a slate of 60-

second spot television ads was proposed as part of Thomas Dewey's campaign, but the

candidate rejected the proposal (Mickelson, 1989).

The 1952 Eisenhower-Stevenson race marked the first extensive use of televised

political advertising. Legendary ad man Rosser Reeves produced 50 one-minute

commercials for the Eisenhower campaign. The ads, which cost $1.5 million to make

and air, featured music by Irving Berlin and animation by Walt Disney (Gronbeck, 1992).

The Democrats, in contrast, used limited spot ads very late in the race, spending only

$77,000 on spot television advertising (Mickelson, 1989). The Eisenhower commercials drastically changed the face of televised political advertising, which up to that point had

meant buying large block of time to air entire candidate speeches (Clark, 1988).

In the 1956 presidential race, both parties spent a combined total of more than $9

million on radio and television advertising (Jeffres, 1986). But those expenditures are a

drop in the bucket compared with modern ad expenditures. Campaign advertising has

become virtually the entire campaign, especially at the presidential level (Squire, 1991).

In the 1992 presidential race alone, the three major candidates spent a total of $133

million on advertising, between two-thirds and three-fourths of their total campaign

budgets (Devlin, 1995). Presidential candidates are not alone in their enormous

advertising budgets. For example, most congressional candidates spend at least 60

percent of their campaign budgets on advertising (Jacobson, 1987).

Current Issues in Political Advertising

Political advertising, television spots in particular, have become an increasingly

important source of political information. Bennett (1989) found that Americans were

slightly less informed about politics in the 1980s than in the 1960s, despite being better

educated. The culprits, Bennett argued, were diminished interest in politics and less

reliance on newspapers, once the main source of political news for the country. Research

has shown that the American electorate gets a significant portion of its information about

candidates and issues from advertising (Weaver & Drew, 1993). In one of the first

studies of the effect of televised campaign advertising, Patterson and McClure (1976)

found that advertising in the 1972 presidential election addressed more of the major

campaign issues than network news programs. Viewers remembered more information from the ads than from televised news about the campaign, despite the fact that they were exposed to the ads for much shorter periods of time. Political advertising brought about a direct and dramatic belief change among voters. The commercials even effectively overcame low-interest voters' avoidance of political information. (McClure & Patterson, 1974).

Researchers have replicated Patterson and McClure's work, finding that ads serve as a major source of information about elections--often more than televised news programs (Kern, 1989; West, 1993; Zhao & Bleske, 1995). Joslyn (1990) argued that campaign ads have educative potential to teach about candidates' personality traits, performance in office, and cultural icons. Martinelli and Chaffee (1995) found that new U.S. citizens learned about where the candidates stood on issues through 1988 political advertising. Just, Crigler, and Wallach (1990) also found that campaign ads helped voters learn about issue positions, even more so than exposure to a lengthy candidate debate. Campaign ads also are seen as an important source of information for disconnected, less informed voters (Owen, 1991).

More and more, messages contained in campaign commercials are negative. Negative ads--also called attack ads--are generally defined as spots that make unflattering or pejorative comments about other candidates' personal qualities, policy stances, or performance on domestic and international affairs (West, 1993). In addition, negative advertising has been used to attack issue campaigns and rival political parties. The use of negative commercials has become the norm in modern political campaigns, with the number of negative ads increasing dramatically in recent years (Merritt, 1984). But negative advertising is nothing new. Gronbeck (1992) traces the phenomenon to the 1796 race, when pamphlets attacked on the characters of Thomas Jefferson and John Adams. Still, most early ads, for example 1952's "Eisenhower answers the nation" spots, were low key, straight forward, and largely factual. Within a decade, the practice had changed.

By 1964, campaign managers and advertising producers "had discovered that the best route to the voter's reflexes is not through his capacity to reason but through his emotions, prejudices, and lingering responses to previous experiences" (Mickelson, 1989, p. 157). That race produced the Johnson campaign's now-famous "Daisy Girl" ad, which featured a girl plucking petals from a daisy. As she counted up, a count-down started for a nuclear bomb launch. The ad, still seen as one of the most negative in televised advertising history, marked the beginning of modern negative political advertising. Goldwater's attack ads--one featured a beer can being thrown out of a moving car in response to reports that Johnson drank beer as he drove--didn't have the same bite or venom (Clark, 1988). Attack advertising reached its peak in the 1964 election, when 40 percent of the ads broadcast were negative. In no other contest to date has the percentage of negative ads been as high (Kaid & Johnston, 1991).

Consultants and campaign managers, pointing to the Johnson campaign's success with negative ads, made attack ads standard practice in elections. Buoyed by research (Garramone, 1985; Garramone & Smith, 1984) and practical evidence showing that people remember and respond to negative political ads, campaign strategists concluded that attack ads work. Although some research has found that such attacks can produce a backlash effect in some circumstances (Garramone, 1984; Roddy & Garramone, 1988), campaigns have not shied away from using such tactics. Kaid and Johnston (1991) found that only 7 percent of the ads in the 1960 presidential contest were negative. From 1968 to 1976, the percentage of negative ads hovered at about 25 percent. Beginning with the 1980 race, however, candidates have routinely attacked in more than 35 percent of their ads (Kaid & Johnston, 1991, Table 1, p. 57). Campaigns at all levels continued to pull out the stops on negative ads after 1988. During the 1988 and 1990 campaigns, attack ads were the norm rather than the exception (Hagstrom & Guskind, 1992). In 1992, about half of each presidential candidate's advertising budget was spent on negative ads (Devlin, 1993).

The Turning Point: 1988

The 1988 presidential race is seen as a watershed election both in terms of candidates' use of negative political advertising and in journalistic coverage of campaign advertising. Although Kaid and Johnston (1991) found that the level of negative campaign spots in the 1988 election was virtually unchanged from the previous two elections, that presidential contest has been called one of the most negative since the McCarthy era (Gronbeck, 1992). About 38 percent of George Bush's ads were negative, while 49 percent of Michael Dukakis ads were negative (Kaid, Gobetz, Garner, Leland, & Scott, 1993).

While the numbers of negative spots may not have increased compared with past presidential races, the media, the candidates, and the public all perceived a saturation of attack ads. Researchers have offered several explanations for this perception. Gronbeck (1992) argues that negative advertising is usually reserved for late in the campaign, beginning a month or two before Election Day. In 1988, negative ads first appeared in mid-summer and came in a steady stream until Election Day. In addition, the ads were seen as more negative and more inaccurate than any used in the past. Jamieson begins her 1992

revision to Packaging the Presidency with this assertion: "Never before in a presidential

campaign have televised ads sponsored by a major party candidate lied so blatantly as in the

campaign of 1988" (1992b, p. xix).

Although Dukakis actually used more campaign ads than Bush (Kaid et al., 1993),

Jamieson and other political pundits put most of the blame for the negativity of the

campaign on Bush. One Bush ad in particular, which attacked Michael Dukakis for being

weak on crime, is universally cited as sounding the wake-up call for journalists and

researchers studying political advertising. The ad, which came to be known as the "Willie

Horton" spot, detailed how one convict raped and robbed while out of prison under the

Massachusetts weekend furlough plan. The commercial implied that Dukakis, the governor

at the time the convict was granted a weekend furlough, was to blame and was soft on

crime. The ad was produced by an "independent" group that supported Bush, the National

Security Political Action Committee, and ran on a few nationwide cable networks (Drew,

1989). Although few people saw the ad featuring Horton, who is black, most major news

outlets ran pictures of Horton and produced news stories featuring the ad and its claims.

The ad, which was widely seen as using racial stereotypes, was uncritically amplified by

news media during the election even though it invited voters to make inaccurate

assumptions about the role Dukakis played in the furlough program (Kern, West, & Alger,

1993). In reality, the furlough program was started by Dukakis' predecessor as governor of

Massachusetts, and Dukakis put an end to the program shortly after the Horton incident

(Jamieson, 1992a).

From the time political advertising first emerged until only recently, it had been a distinct part of campaigns, separate from news coverage and other campaign events. But in 1988, ads began to shape news coverage routinely for the first time. Republicans, largely through advertising, defined campaign issues for the media and voters in the 1988 race, as well as for Dukakis. The Bush camp, through its ads, even defined the vocabulary used by the news media in covering the campaign. Jamieson (1992a) points to the famous "Willie Horton" ad as a vivid example. While Horton's name was listed as William on all of his official records and he went by the name William, the commercial identified him as "Willie," which Jamieson argues brings to mind the nicknames white slave owners gave their black slaves. Virtually all news organizations referred to him as "Willie" during the 1988 election. "Where news once contextualized ads, visually evocative and easily edited oppositional ads backed by reinforcing candidate speeches and pseudo-events now have the capacity to shape the language for news" (Jamieson, 1992a, p. 135).

Journalist Response: The Ad Cops are Deputized

Journalists are trained to think of themselves as the public's "watchdogs," exposing corruption and ensuring that government functions efficiently and in the public's best interests. In theory, journalists covering campaigns expose character flaws and inaccurate candidate claims in an attempt to help voters make the most informed choice on Election Day. This "watchdog" role recently has been extended to political advertising.

Although campaign coverage by news organizations first arose after George Washington left office in 1796 (Stebenne, 1993), journalists have only recently begun reporting on political advertising. Reporters first made news out of political advertising

in the 1964 Johnson-Goldwater race, reporting on Johnson's "Daisy Girl" attack ad. The

commercial was broadcast only once, on September 7, 1964 (Jamieson, 1992b). But all

three networks re-broadcast the entire ad in their nightly newscasts (West, 1993). Until

recently, however, political advertising rarely was deemed a subject to be covered on the

same level as debates and campaign appearances, which receive almost daily

examination. A few stories included discussions of candidates' advertising strategy, and

a few ad critiques were produced. But those "were so tame as to be almost worthless"

(Alter, 1990). Just before the 1992 presidential election, Rachlin wrote of this dearth of

coverage: "Perhaps the most specific and tangible criticism of media coverage of past

campaigns has been that the media didn't do sufficient analytical evaluation of candidate

advertising" (1992, p. 33). But the increasing number of negative spots and the enormous

budgets spent on advertising in the 1980s, especially 1988, caused journalists to take

notice.

Journalists seemed almost embarrassed by missing the value of ads in the Bush-

Dukakis race and stumbling in their role as public watchdog. John Funk, a political

reporter for The Plain Dealer in Cleveland wrote: "That it took the Willie Horton spots of

the 1988 presidential campaign to alert print journalists to the consequences of these

unchallenged media campaigns underscores how out of touch we are with the society we

pretend to serve" (Wolinsky, Sparks, Funk, Rooney, Lyon, & Sweet, 1991, p. 24). The

Associated Press' John Wholman echoed Funk's critique of media performance in

previous campaigns: "One lesson from 1988 was that we were spending too much time on the candidate's day and not enough on the paid political advertising that was a main

source of information for many, if not most, Americans" (quoted in Rachlin, 1992, p. 33).

Following the Bush-Dukakis contest, media commentators challenged their peers

to do a better job of policing political advertising (Broder, 1989; Hinerfeld, 1990). Even

the advertising industry urged changes. For example, Advertising Age suggested that the

Advertising Council prepare public service announcements reminding voters that political

commercials are almost never the whole truth (Garfield, 1990). Reformers argued that it

was the news media's role as public watchdog to force the candidates to behave more

responsibility in their ads (Smith, 1990). The solution, they argued, was to deputize

journalists, in effect creating an elite core of "ad cops" to patrol the campaign advertising

beat. Not only did news organizations become ad police, identifying suspected offenders,

they also served as prosecutors, presenting to the voters arguments on how the advertising

was false or misleading.

The form of choice to present these arguments were "adwatches," defined as

"media critiques of candidate ads designed to inform the public about truthful or

misleading advertising claims" (Kaid, McKinnon, & Tedesco, 1995, p. 3). The term

adwatch has been used to describe everything from general news stories about overall

advertising tactics in a campaign to critiques of claims made in one or more specific

campaign commercials. The latter, also called "truth boxes" or "reality checks," became

the method of choice for many news outlets critiquing ads.[2] Journalists saw the new

technique as a wrench they could hurl at the powerful political ad machines. In this view,

---

[2] This research uses the term adwatch as synonymous with "truth boxes" to refer only to specific critiques of ad claims.

adwatches could "institutionalize scrutiny of campaign ads and highlight distortions and inaccuracies for otherwise unsuspecting viewers and readers" (Lichter & Noyes, 1995, p. 137).

The first adwatches appeared in a limited number of regional media outlets during the 1990 congressional and statewide races. Adwatches appeared in newspapers, in magazines, on radio, and on television. During that election, Alter (1990) observed that political reporters were spending more time in the library checking out ad claims than on the stump. The new technique generated much attention among the journalistic community. Trade magazines and publications wrote about news organizations' success with adwatches, and a Barone Center report praised early adwatches, dubbing them a political and commercial success (Hume, 1991).

With the trial run in 1990, journalists were ready to use adwatches widely in the 1992 presidential race. "The news media entered the election year with a distinct 'state of mind,' which was clearly a product of much soul-searching in the aftermath of a performance in 1988 that was almost universally condemned as dismal" (Alger, 1994). A survey taken before the 1992 election found that 60 percent of local television news directors planned to expand coverage of the accuracy of local political advertising (Wicks & Kern, 1993).

Some suggest that journalists took aim at campaign advertising primarily because they were feeling "out of the loop." Roger Ailes, a media adviser to George Bush, said the change in journalists' attitudes toward covering political advertising was brought about because "journalists, who had begun to feel ignored, decided to go on the offensive" (Wolinsky et al., 1991, p. 27). Candidates and their campaign managers see political ads as a form of campaign communication that is entirely within their control, whereas other forms of political communication--such as speeches and debates--are filtered through the channels that carry them. As candidates turned to more direct communication with the voters, journalists began to scrutinize these messages just as they had in the past with campaign speeches or news conferences. Journalists made no bones about their desire to take back the spotlight from campaign commercials. For example, after an onslaught of political ads in California state races, the <u>Los Angeles Times</u> moved to "balance the equation" with truth boxes. Leo C. Wolinsky, the paper's political editor, said the analyses were intended to "embarrass campaigns into more accurately portraying the candidates and their positions" (Wolinsky et al., 1991, p. 22).

Midway through the 1992 presidential contest, a survey found that 85 percent of reporters and editors approved of news coverage of political commercials (Times Mirror, 1992). After the election, that approval rating dropped only slightly, to 77 percent favoring of ad coverage. Most respondents said they saw "truth-telling" as a legitimate role for journalists. Many reporters and editors surveyed said they thought adwatches influenced the type of advertising that candidates used in the race. One television newsman told the researchers in 1992 that such propaganda debunking "is the primary reason why no Willie Horton ads or their cousins have appeared in this campaign. Our coverage is keeping the bastards honest" (Times Mirror, 1993, p. 3). Even those who were wary of the media's broad new role at least favored the technique to expose outright "lies" in ads (Lichter & Noyes, 1995).

The move to ad "truth squads" was driven not only by news organizations, but also by the public. Media critic Jonathan Alter described two rebellions in American politics in the early 1990s: one, against politics as usual, and the second against media as usual (quoted in Pease, 1992). The whole system of modern campaign coverage was under attack in 1992. Not only were voters anti-government, they were also anti-media. "The model of campaign coverage that had developed over the past four decades had itself come under mounting criticism, some from the very same journalists, editors, pollsters, pundits and politicians who had shaped it, and, perhaps more importantly, from the electorate itself" (Stebenne, 1993, p. 90). Anecdotal evidence suggests that the public was quite aware of the new role the media took on in response to attack advertising's increasingly prominent role in the campaign. In a focus group conducted by Alger, Kern, and West (1993) one participant stated: "There's one thing about the media in this election, I think more so that, when they know an ad is misleading, they come out and tell ya, more during this campaign than in previous ones. You know, they'll tell you why it is that it's misleading, and they'll tell you the source where they got the information" (p. 12).

By 1992, the ad check format had been so widely used that journalists were using "truth squad" as a verb in casual conversation. Jerry Hagstrom, a National Journal contributing editor, said in a 1992 panel discussion that he believed the adwatches were having an impact: "We believe that the campaigns are less likely to make errors in advertising if they know they're being tracked for accuracy." But Columbia University history professor Henry Graff immediately countered this assertion: "On this truth squad business, I wonder who's listening?" (Media Scoreboard, Round 3, p. 90).

The Problem with Adwatches

Ironically, journalists' efforts to police misleading campaign commercials may have backfired. Kaid et al. (1993) argue that news coverage of advertising legitimizes ads as an information source in the minds of voters and to broadens the audience exposed to the message. "Increased coverage by television news may be an important reason for the growing importance of television ads" (p. 281). Consultants, realizing this, have begun to construct ads that they know will receive news coverage. "You get a 30 to 40 percent bump out of ads by getting on the news," Ailes said. "You get more viewers, you get credibility" (quoted in West, 1993, p. 14). It could be argued that television and other media have increased coverage because of the growing importance of political ads, with each feeding off the other in an upward spiral. While journalists began covering ads because of the increasing negativity, that coverage only fueled more negative ads, Ailes said. Because the media love to cover attacks, "if you need coverage, you attack, and you will get coverage" (quoted in Runkel, 1989).

Political consultants also began to use the "facts" presented in adwatches as ammunition in their counter-attack ads, taking information that might never have been seen by a wide audience and running it repeatedly in ads placed in high-profile time slots (National Journal, 1990). In an ironic twist, journalists themselves often were "misquoted" in the ads as the campaigns flashed headlines and quoted reporting from the news media out of context (Goodman, 1990; Ansolabehere & Iyengar, 1995).

In addition, adwatches almost always focused on negative ads, which made voters see the campaigns as more negative than they actually were. This negative picture may have a demobilizing effect on the electorate in the long run. Garramone, Atkin, Pinkleton, and Cole (1990) found that exposure to negative ads did not depress political participation. But Ansolabehere. Iyengar, Simon, and Valentino (1994) found just the opposite. That study found that exposure to negative advertisements reduced subjects' intentions to vote by 5 percent. In addition, the negative campaign exposure decreased political efficacy and made voters more cynical, the researchers found.

But even more serious, some media critics contend, is the change that adwatches and other new forms of political "analysis" represent in the traditional role of the press. Lichter and Noyes (1995) see this new form of journalism as a sharp departure from the "objective" coverage of political contests that reporters had sought for decades prior to 1992. Journalists used to see their job as informing the public, getting the facts straight and reporting what politicians said and did. Today, Lichter contends, "the priorities have been reversed, and journalists think their main job is to tell the public that the politicians are fooling them and explain how" (quoted in Hernandez, 1996, p. 12). Rosenstiel (1993) argued that this new role transformed the relationship between the news media and candidates by changing the political reporter from "a color commentator up in the booth to a referee down on the field," meaning the press not only reflected events, but also shaped them (p. 273). Fallows (1996) also castigates reporters for substituting reporting with political "analysis," which has served to perpetuate an overly suspicious view of candidates' motives.

Finally, Lichter and Noyes contend, adwatches represented a blending of commentary and news that, although eschewed in the past, was rationalized as "truth-telling" and seen as a public service. "The news went boldly where only editorials had gone before, and news organizations instituted 'adwatches' and 'reality checks' to keep them honest. The result was some of the least balanced, most negative, and most opinionated coverage in the era of mediated elections" (Lichter & Noyes, 1995, xvii). The authors also argue that adwatches rarely corrected falsehoods but merely replaced the campaign's interpretation of ambiguous "facts" with the writer's own interpretations. "By painting with broad brush strokes . . . the networks' 'ad police' sometimes resembled vigilantes more than sheriffs" (Lichter & Noyes, 1995, p. 139). Patterson (1993) reminds journalists that "news and truth are not the same thing" (p. 29). Jay Rosen, a New York University professor often called the father of "public journalism," shares Patterson's view. Fact-checking has been put on the back burner in recent elections as reporters became more eager to provide "analysis." According to Rosen, adwatches "became new forums for reporters to show their savviness" (quoted in Canellos, 1996, p. 7).

Problem Definition

In reflecting on the outlook for attack ads, Roddy and Garramone (1988) argued that the major determinant of the future of negative ads should be the perceived effectiveness of attack ads in persuading voters. The same argument could be made about adwatches. While political pundits and media critics debate whether adwatches are the proper role for journalists to play in a campaign, a key question mass communication researchers should be asking is whether and how the ad checks work. Ansolabehere and

Iyengar (1995) describe the issue as follows: "If adwatches live up to their promise, they will make voters generally less susceptible to campaign advertising and less supportive of candidates who engage in deceptive advertising" (p. 137). Political consultants and campaign managers say they wouldn't use negative advertising if it were not an effective tool. Adwatch research should take that same approach, asking whether this new form of political coverage is effective in countering and filtering the messages in political advertising--the role journalists envisioned when they began policing ads.

To date, only a few studies have examined adwatches. Even fewer studies have explored the effects adwatches have on voters. This study aims to fill this gap. In particular, this research is designed to take a new approach to understanding the effects exposure to adwatches has on voters. The few studies that have begun to assess adwatch effects have produced mixed results.

The current study attempts to make sense of these conflicting findings by examining adwatches from an individual differences perspective. Meadow (1989) lamented that research on political campaigns had only undergone "a modest evolution from hypodermic thinking to more sophisticated models of persuasion that recognize the interaction between campaign messages and the voter" (p. 271). He urged more researchers to examine this interaction. This research heeds his call.

The research also strives to break ground by examining adwatches as persuasive messages, specifically by applying the Elaboration Likelihood Model (ELM) of persuasion to test adwatch effects. Journalists, guided by the principle of objectivity, might bristle at the classification of adwatches--which they see as "truth boxes"--as persuasion. But Lichter and Noyes (1995), Patterson (1993), and other media observers argue that adwatches have moved political coverage out of its "objective" stance into the realm of persuasion. The current study uses an experimental design to explain the influence of moderating variables--specifically the need for cognition, argument quality, and source credibility--on voters' attitudes toward political advertisements and candidates after exposure to commercials and adwatches that critique them.

The next chapter describes the theoretical framework that forms the basis of this study. In particular, adwatch research and literature on the ELM is reviewed. Hypotheses suggested by this literature are presented at the end of Chapter II. The method used to test the hypotheses, including a detailed description of the independent and dependent variables, is described in the third chapter. Results of the data analysis are presented in Chapter IV. The study's final chapter presents a summation of the results, limitations of the study, a discussion of the findings, possible practical implications of the findings for journalists, and suggestions for future research.

CHAPTER II
LITERATURE REVIEW

The effects of media messages have been a key component of mass communication research since the discipline began. Researchers have looked at a variety of factors to measure media effects, including awareness of messages and learning from messages. A third way of studying media effects has been to define effects in terms of persuasion (Thorson & Coyle, 1994). This research will examine adwatch effects in a persuasive context. After a review of the scant research to date on adwatches, persuasion theories as they can be applied to advertising and adwatches will be discussed. Next, the Elaboration Likelihood Model (ELM) of persuasion will be reviewed. One moderating variable that has been used in that model, the need for cognition, will be explained in detail because of its central role in this study. The chapter concludes with a set of research hypotheses derived from the theoretical framework.

Adwatch Research

Conventional wisdom holds that news reports provide a frame in which viewers understand ads by setting the context. If the news accounts are inconsistent with the ad, the ad is considered less effective. But if the messages are consistent, both are magnified (Jamieson, 1992a). It is still unclear whether coverage of political advertising, adwatches in particular, fits that pattern. Studies of general news coverage of political advertising are relatively new, and studies of adwatches in particular are in their infancy. To date, only a handful of studies have examined this emerging form of political communication.

Most adwatch research has focused on the presidential level (Kern et al., 1993; West, Kern, & Alger, 1992; Kern & Just, 1994; McKinnon, Kaid, Murphy & Acree, 1996; Alger et al., 1993; Kaid et al., 1995; Cappella & Jamieson, 1994). Only two studies have examined adwatches at the statewide level (Pfau & Louden, 1994; O'Sullivan & Geiger, 1995). Since 1990, many local newspapers of all sizes have followed the lead of The Miami Herald, publishing adwatches of candidate ads for local races. To date, no published research has examined adwatches for local races. Researchers have used a variety of methods--content analyses, surveys, and experiments-- to study adwatches. Studies using each of these methods, and the findings produced, will be discussed in turn.

Content Analyses

Many of the adwatch studies have used content analyses to examine the occurrence and type of political adwatches produced by the news media. The first content analysis of political advertising coverage appeared in 1975. In a study of newspaper advertising coverage during the 1972 presidential race, Bowers (1975) found few print media articles about advertising. The few that were published dealt with ad strategies, not the content of a specific ad or ads.

Kaid et al. (1993) conducted the first content analysis of televised news coverage of political advertising. After reviewing 1,802 network television news stories for presidential contests from 1972 to 1988, the researchers documented a sharp increase in the number of stories mentioning or dealing solely with campaign advertising.[1] Only 13

network news stories mentioned candidate commercials in 1972. That number jumped to

79 in 1988, more than three times as the election with the next highest number of

advertising-related news stories, 1980 (see Kaid et al., 1993, Table 1, p. 278). Most of

these stories were not adwatches--used in this study to describe a "fact-based" critique of

one or more specific ads--but merely mentioned advertising in routine campaign reports.

In fact, only 19 of the stories--15 percent of the total 131 identified by the researchers as

dealing with political commercials--focused exclusively on campaign advertising. Nearly

half of those 19 were broadcast during the 1988 contest alone. The study also found that

networks were more likely to cover negative ads than positive ones in the 1988 race.

More than 77 percent of the advertising stories broadcast that year contained a clip from a

negative ad, while only 35 percent of the stories aired part or all of a positive ad.[2]

Kaid et al. (1995) extended their research to include the 1992 race. Television

news directors had professed intentions before the election to expand coverage of

political advertising. But Kaid's follow-up study showed a drop in the number of

network adwatch segments in 1992. The researchers examined all political advertising

features appearing on the three networks from Labor Day (September 6) to Election Day

(November 2), 1992, and found 44 feature stories that discussed candidate advertising.[3]

The study examined slant of coverage, finding more than half of the features (56.8

[1] The study coded information from ABC, CBS, and NBC nightly newscasts obtained
from the Vanderbilt Television News Index and Abstracts and videotapes of the
newscasts. The study, which relied on six graduate assistants as coders, reported an
average intercoder reliability of +.87.
[2] Several news stories broadcast parts of more than one advertisement.
[3] Average intercoder reliability was +.91.

percent) neutral, 36.4 percent with a negative slant, and only 6.3 percent with a positive

slant. Again, networks were most likely to critique negative ads, with nearly half (47.7

percent) of the news features discussing negative ads while 29.5 percent focused on

positive ads.[4] Stories about independent candidate Ross Perot's ads dominated the

network coverage. Perot ads accounted for 43.2 percent of the stories; George Bush ads

were featured in 20.5 percent; and Bill Clinton ads were the focus of 6.8 percent of the

stories.[5]

McKinnon et al. (1996), a group that included Kaid, took the same approach in

analyzing newspaper adwatches. The researchers reviewed adwatches printed in five

newspapers during the 1992 presidential, congressional and Senate races.[6] The

researchers identified 126 stories (63 features on advertising and 59 adwatches or "truth

boxes," and four combination articles). The findings paralleled those of network ad

coverage. For example, the majority of newspaper articles (62 percent) focused on a

negative ads, while 33 percent examined positive ads. Also, the vast majority of the

advertising coverage (87 percent of the stories) was coded as neutral, while 10 percent

were coded as having a negative slant and 3 percent as having a positive slant.

Interestingly, the newspaper coverage of advertising dealt not with local races, where

newspaper articles could potentially have a great effect on voters, but with national and

[4] The remaining 22.8 percent of the adwatches could not be identified as either negative or positive.
[5] The remaining 26.9 percent did not discuss a specific ad or discussed a combination of candidate ads.
[6] The papers, selected to achieve regional distribution and to cover areas in which races for both the House of Representatives and Senate were taking place were: Los Angeles Times, The New York Times, The Miami Herald, Chicago Tribune, and Washington Post. Average intercoder reliability for the study was +.90.

statewide contests. About 70 percent of the articles analyzed ads by presidential

candidates and 22 percent focused on ads in Senate races. Advertising stories on House

races, other contests, and a combination of races accounted for only 8 percent of the total.

About 76 percent of the stories included either all or part of the advertising copy when

critiquing the ad. McKinnon et al. looked only at ad coverage during the 1992

presidential race, meaning no trend analysis could be performed for newspapers as had

been done by Kaid et al. (1995).

Kern et al. (1993) also studied news coverage of 1992 presidential advertising,

using content analysis to examine both ads and adwatches. Kern and her colleagues used

a broader set of adwatches than was used in either of the content analyses described

above. The researchers analyzed articles and ads from the three television networks,

CNN, local television newscasts, and newspaper coverage in four markets.[7] The review

found 93 nationally televised advertising stories during the campaign. Twenty-five of the

stories were aired during the primary season (January to June 6), 21 during the summer

months, and 47 during the general election (September 1 through Election Day). During

the primary season, only 50 percent of the stories covering political advertising tried to

evaluate the ads as opposed to describing simply what the commercials said. In the

general election, 76 percent of the advertising stories evaluated the ads. In contrast to

Kaid's findings, Kern discovered that Perot ads actually received less scrutiny from the

media because his ads were evaluated mainly by the less critical standard of the primary

---

[7] The local newscast and newspaper markets were chosen to cover all regions of the
country and range from small to large markets. That criteria left the researchers with
Fargo, South Dakota; Moorhead, Minnesota; Boston; and Los Angeles. No intercoder
reliability was reported in the study.

season. The researchers also found that the ads themselves were aired in more than half

of the 1992 televised stories about advertising, which could potentially amplify candidate

advertising messages.

Surveys

Kern et al. (1993) went beyond analyzing content to look at public opinion

surveys conducted in four local markets in which advertisements and ad coverage were

studied. To date, it is the only known study to use a survey to examine the influence of

adwatches on voters.[8] Telephone surveys were conducted with more than 4,000

individuals in the four markets during the primary season, the summer, and the general

campaign.

About half of the respondents reported seeing news stories on political advertising

during the spring and summer, while more than 60 percent said they had seen news

coverage of advertising during the October survey. Most respondents said they saw this

coverage on television. On average, about 15 percent of the respondents said the

coverage was very helpful, 40 percent classified it as somewhat helpful, and about 45

percent said the coverage was not helpful.[9] These rankings showed that voters saw

adwatches as a source of political information equal to ads themselves and to general

campaign news. Voters also reported "that adwatches were a more significant information

source than the 'newest' information phenomenon of the 1992 election campaign, the

extended news format" (Kern et al., 1993, p. 19). The researchers concluded that

---

[8] West, Kern, and Alger (1992) also reported survey results in their findings. The researchers used the same data set reported in the Kern et al. study.
[9] This is a broad generalization of the findings. For specific figures for each market on during each of the survey periods see Kern et al. (1993) Table 1.

exposure to adwatches caused voters to evaluate the leadership abilities of Bush and Clinton more positively.

Experimental Designs

Researchers have recently moved beyond simply describing what adwatches look like and when they appear. Studies have begun to ask whether adwatches are actually doing what journalists intend--that is making voters more critical of campaign advertisements and the claims they make. While the survey conducted by Kern et al. (1993) provides a good starting point for assessing the influence newspaper adwatches have on attitudes toward candidates, experimental designs often provide a clearer picture of media effects. A few recent studies, all published since 1994, have used experimental designs to examine the effects of adwatch exposure on voter attitudes toward campaign ads and candidates.

Cappella and Jamieson (1994) conducted a controlled field experiment to examine the effects of adwatches on attitudes toward the source of the ad, the target of the ad, the ad itself, and recall and interpretation of the ad's content. The stimulus, a televised Pat Buchanan ad that ran during the 1992 Michigan primary, attacked George Bush and his advisers. The researchers recruited 165 subjects from a wide range of racial, age, and educational groups in 11 U.S. cities. The study examined manipulations of varying number of exposures to the ad, adwatch production techniques used to "correct" the ad, and the number of days between viewing the adwatch and being asked to evaluate the Buchanan ad. Comparing the experimental conditions with a control group showed that exposure to an adwatch caused subjects to view the targeted ad as less fair and less important. In addition, those viewing a televised adwatch held more negative attitudes toward Buchanan than subjects in the control group. The adwatches had no effect, however, on the object of the attack (Bush) nor on interpretation of the ad's content.

An interesting finding produced by the Cappella and Jamieson experiment was that subjects who saw the adwatches before being exposed to the Buchanan ad were more critical of the ad than those who saw the adwatch after the political ad. "Once political ads have had the opportunity to work on the audience, and the opportunity to frame the issue has passed, the effects of later adwatches might be less consequential," the researchers conclude (p. 358). However, most adwatches don't appear until after an ad has been aired or printed. While Cappella and Jamieson urge the news media to be "out ahead of the political image-makers with their critical evaluations," journalists might have a hard time reacting to an event that has not yet occurred. In addition, campaign managers would soon learn to produce an ad, turn it over to the media for a critique, wait for the news story to appear, and never place the ad, instead opting for the "free" media exposure provided by the news organization. This practice would be especially attractive to campaigns if adwatches can have a "boomerang" effect, causing people to hold more positive views of the ad and the sponsoring candidate instead of invoking more critical evaluations as journalists intend.

This "boomerang" effect was first documented by Pfau and Louden (1994). In contrast to Cappella and Jamieson's findings, the researchers found that adwatches were not effective in making voters more "savvy consumers" of political advertising claims. Pfau and Louden (1994) examined the effect of different televised adwatch formats in deflecting the influence of targeted political attack ads. The experiment, which used 340 Wake Forest University students as subjects, examined the effectiveness of different formats of televised adwatches in checking two ads aired in the 1992 North Carolina gubernatorial race.

Subjects who viewed a full-screen rebroadcast of 15 seconds of the ad as part of the adwatch actually held a more positive emotional response to the candidate sponsoring the ad, held a more positive attitude toward the commercial, and reported being more likely to vote for the commercial's sponsoring candidate than subjects in the control group. Their conclusion was that adwatches using a full-screen rebroadcast of the ad--a common technique among many television news organizations--had a "boomerang" effect. Instead of casting the television commercial in a negative light, rebroadcasting even part of the ad during the adwatch segment reinforced the ad's content, allowing viewers to recall more of the commercial and to hold a more positive attitude toward the ad and its sponsoring candidate. The boomerang was most pronounced among female viewers.

Part of the problem, the researchers concluded, what that subjects had trouble distinguishing a news report about an ad from the ad itself. Boot (1989) echoed this thinking while writing about the coverage of the Bush-Dukakis contest: "Confusion was compounded in 1988 by a proliferation of television news reports about commercials, of commercials inspired by news reports, and of commercials about commercials" (p. 29).

Ansolabehere and Iyengar (1995) also documented the potential for adwatches to backfire or boomerang. In three experiments, which exposed subjects to actual CNN adwatch stories from the 1992 presidential contest, the researchers asked 330 subjects to rate the candidates according to several traits--intelligence, integrity, diligence, and compassion--and to indicate which candidate they would be more likely to vote for. In each case, the candidates whose advertisements were criticized gained support. Adwatches aimed at negative commercials seemed to give the candidates an even bigger boost, according to the study. Exposure to an adwatch also caused non-partisan voters to register a significant increase in their sense of alienation and cynicism.[10]

Ansolabehere and Iyengar concluded that the boomerang was the result of CNN's tactic of repeating the ads' themes in their adwatches. Repeating the ad's content caused the adwatch to strengthen recall of the ad claims, making the favorable information about the candidate more accessible in memory. The authors conclude:

> This new form of campaign journalism has a long way to
> go before it realizes its stated objectivity of empowering
> voters. It becomes almost amusing to see how exposure to
> adwatch reports boosts support for the "targeted" advertiser
> and therefore plays into the hands of the candidates
> (Ansolabehere and Iyengar, 1995, p. 15).

While these findings seem vastly different from the Cappella and Jamieson (1994) study described above, Jamieson has argued the results actually are consistent with her research. The adwatches used in Ansolabehere and Iyengar's laboratory experiment concluded that the ads being reviewed were basically true, therefore the respondents thought more highly of the candidates. In contrast, the adwatches used in the Cappella and Jamieson experiment concluded the ad was deceptive, causing respondents to think less of the candidate. Therefore, the content of the adwatches is what drove the different

---

[10] Adwatch exposure had no such effect on Republican and Democratic subjects.

findings, she argued. "Both of us have found that the adwatches work as they were intended--they contextualize the ad," Jamieson said in a recent television interview (quoted in Shaw, 1996).

But discrepant findings on adwatch effects have been produced by other studies. Pfau and Burgoon's (1988) work on inoculation messages suggested that newspaper adwatches might blunt the effectiveness of attack ads. Milburn and Brown's (1995) experimental study concluded that adwatch columns in the 1992 presidential race may have helped viewers critically process advertising information. Geiger (1993), in contrast, found that truth boxes produced weak to no effects about candidate evaluations. The small effects that were found showed that over time, truth boxes gave a subtle boost to the candidate's image, regardless whether the truth box information supported or refuted the claims of the ad being critiqued. Geiger urged more research on adwatches, particularly on the content of the adwatches themselves.

O'Sullivan and Geiger (1995) followed that suggestion and examined whether varying the content of an adwatch produced different effects on voters' perceptions of candidates. Using an experimental method with 112 undergraduate students as subjects, the researchers studied for four statewide races. O'Sullivan and Geiger manipulated whether the adwatch articles confirmed or contradicted a candidate's ad claims and claims made in an opponent's ad. Subjects who were exposed to an adwatch supporting a candidate's attack on an opponent and subjects exposed to an adwatch contradicting an opponent's attack gave the candidate significantly higher marks for character, ability, and liking. In contrast, when adwatches contradicted a candidate's attack ad or supported an opponent's attack ad, evaluations of the candidate's character, ability, and liking were significantly lower. "This indicates that newspaper critiques of attack ads can be a powerful determinant of how the ads affect people's assessments of candidates" (O'Sullivan & Geiger, 1995, p. 780). The findings also would seem to explain the different effects of adwatch exposure reported by Cappella and Jamieson (1994) and Ansolabehere and Iyengar (1995), discussed above.

In sum, research on adwatch effects has produced mixed results. While some studies have found that exposure to adwatches can affect attitudes toward political advertisements and the sponsoring candidate, other studies have found just the opposite.

A New Approach

Insight into the mixed findings produced by past adwatch effects studies might be gained by examining adwatches using persuasion theories, specifically the Elaboration Likelihood Model of persuasion. This model suggests an explanation for the discrepancies in findings from previous adwatch research: Adwatches may not affect all people the same way. No study to date has examined adwatch effects in light of individual differences. Looking at differences in the individuals, especially differences in cognitive processing of the persuasive messages they receive, should provide clues to the conflicting findings produced by experimental tests of adwatch effects to date.

Persuasion research provides a solid framework in which to study advertising. Persuasion is aimed at changing beliefs, the cognitive component of attitudes. Persuasive messages, therefore, present information aimed at changing attitudes. Advertising--whether political, product, or issue-oriented--all has the same goal: to change attitudes.

In turn, producers of the ads hope changes in attitudes will translate into changes in behavior (Jeffres, 1986). Jamieson and Campbell (1992) argue that all news, entertainment, and advertising messages contain a persuasive component. Of the three, advertising's persuasive function is the most overt. "The end of advertising is more likely to be explicit action. Here ads are more akin to editorials, which urge action, than other sorts of (news or entertainment) content surrounding them" (p. 158).

Understanding how and why attitudes change in response to a campaign ad is key to examining the effectiveness of political advertising. The goal of a political ad, as with any other persuasive message, is to convince the audience to adopt the position advocated--seeing the candidate in a positive light and, increasingly, the opponent in a negative light. Campaign managers hope that the change in attitudes produced by ads will have a direct result in the voting booth, although scores of studies have shown that behavior doesn't always follow attitude change brought on by campaigns (for example, McGuire, 1989).

While few would debate the classification of political advertising as persuasion, labeling adwatches as persuasion might give some--especially working journalists--pause. Journalists producing adwatches might argue that adwatches are not persuasion, which has been classified as a form of propaganda. Instead, they might argue, adwatches have the same function of all other types of news--to inform. Therefore, adwatches should be seen as education because the news articles convey "objective facts" about claims made in the ads. Some media observers discount this claim of objectivity in general. Jamieson and Campbell (1992) argue that all news functions as persuasion by deciding what is covered and how it is presented. "News coverage becomes persuasion when language is used to create insinuations, when news coverage supports or opposes governmental policies, and when self-censorship suppresses certain kinds of news stories" (p. 93).

Others argue that while some news coverage can make a claim of "objectivity," adwatches don't fit in that category. With adwatches, news organizations attempt to persuade audiences that the information contained in the political advertisement under review is, in most cases, misleading or an outright falsehood. Next, adwatches attempt to persuade voters that the information provided in the adwatch is the truth. In this regard, adwatches are comparable to other persuasive features in the news media, such as movie reviews or editorials. John Funk, a reporter who wrote adwatches for The Plain Dealer in Cleveland during the 1990 elections, is a working journalist who voiced this opinion: "The truth boxes are not news stories, they are critiques" (Wolinsky et al., 1991, p. 24). Lichter and Noyes (1995) also bristle at the notion that adwatches can provide some sort of "objective" account of the "truth." They provide several incidences of adwatches "misinterpreting" the facts they were supposed to correct. The examples, Lichter and Noyes argue,

> clearly cast doubt on the assumptions behind TV's "Ad Watch" style of reporting. One of the criticisms of campaign ads was that the "facts" they claimed to provide were illusory, built upon a foundation of shaky evidence. The conceit was that journalists could replace the ad-makers' illusions with a certifiable reality (p. 146.)

Adwatches can be seen as similar to counter-attack advertising, which attempts to refute the claims made in an attack ad. In fact, arguments made in adwatches routinely are picked up by the opposing campaign and used verbatim in response advertising, providing more "fodder for the politicians" (Wolinsky et al., 1991, p. 28). The fact that journalists often find information used as ammunition in counter-attack ads shows the persuasive potential of the information contained in adwatches (Ansolabehere & Iyengar, 1995).

While many argue that adwatches are persuasion or at least have a persuasive component, persuasion theories provide a legitimate way of looking at adwatches for yet another reason. Adwatches, even if not persuasion in their own right, are aimed at advertising, which is uniformly classified as persuasion. Past adwatch studies have measured effectiveness of adwatches using advertisement evaluation as the dependent measure. Therefore, persuasion literature provides a solid theoretical framework for examining adwatch effects.

Persuasion Research: A Brief History

For decades, researchers have focused on the cognitive responses of individuals exposed to persuasive messages. Persuasion studies grew from Lasswell's research on propaganda during World War I. Lasswell defined propaganda as "influencing human action by the manipulation of representations" and argued that it included both advertising and publicity (Lasswell, 1937, p. 521). Later, researchers began distinguishing between persuasion and propaganda, with the latter taking on a more sinister connotation.

From the 1920s through the 1960s, many researchers in several fields studied the psychology of persuasion. McGuire (1969) identified five steps in the persuasion process: attention, comprehension, yielding, retention, and action (or overt behavior).

Despite hundreds of studies produced in these four decades, research failed to link

changes in attitudes to changes in behaviors, and few generalizations were made from the

findings. As a result, researchers' interest in persuasion began to wane. But in the late

1970s, a renewed optimism invigorated persuasion and attitude research as new methods

emerged and new researchers began to find evidence for a link between attitudes and

behaviors (Cialdini, Petty & Cacioppo, 1981).

Social psychologists have developed scores of persuasion models in the past 50

years. Petty and Cacioppo (1981) identified seven major approaches in examining

persuasion and attitude change, each focusing on a different process. From the first

developed to the most recent, these models are: 1) those that stress basic learning

principles, such as condition with rewards and punishment; 2) message learning

approaches developed at Yale University; 3) perceptual-judgmental theories of

persuasion, such as social judgment theory; 4) those that stress human motives as they

relate to attitude change; 5) information processing approaches, which examine how

inferences about behavior shape attitudes; 6) mathematical models calculating how

persuasive messages are integrated into overall attitudes; and 7) those models that stress

information that people generate themselves in response to persuasion.

Until the early 1980s, theories of attitude change and formation in response to

persuasive messages were divided into two categories. Early attitude change theorists

viewed persuasion in one of two ways. One camp saw persuasion as a rational process in

which an individual adopted a position after receiving and yielding to supporting

arguments from a source (for example, McGuire, 1969). These researchers tied the persuasion process to a person's thoughtful consideration of issue-relevant arguments. Others contended that persuasion was simpler, resulting from a person's opinion about the source advocating a position or about other cues in the persuasive situation (for example, Osgood & Tannenbaum, 1955). Until the mid 1970s, the dominant model of the persuasion process featured an individual actively processing message content of a persuasive communication (Fishbein & Ajzen, 1981). This was often termed the "high, involvement/verbal response model" (Alwitt & Mitchell, 1985, p. 273).

By the 1970s, however, researchers began to stress the interaction between the two types of persuasion. Studies began to document that different people were more likely to process information in different ways and that processing could vary depending on the situation. For example, Norman (1976) found that audiences looked to the number and quality of arguments when deciding whether to trust an "expert" source, while message characteristics did not affect attitudes when the persuasion came from an "attractive" source (see also Mills & Harvey, 1972). However, these researchers looked at persuasive effects as being constant in all subjects and did not examine possible individual differences among audience members.

The Elaboration Likelihood Model of Persuasion

The Elaboration Likelihood Model (ELM) of persuasion, developed by Petty and Cacioppo (1981, 1986a) as a "general theory of attitude change," was devised to help make sense of conflicting theories of attitude change in social psychology research. The ELM brought together source, message, and audience characteristics emphasized in past approaches to attitude change into one model (Petty, Kasmer, Haugtvedt, & Cacioppo,

1987). The ELM has become increasingly popular in social, consumer behavior and communications research in the past decade, primarily because of its usefulness in understanding advertising and other communication effects.

The model is based on the assumption that people want to hold correct attitudes, and people can arrive at those attitudes in a number of ways. Petty and Cacioppo (1986a) define attitude as "general evaluations people hold in regard to themselves, other people, objects, and issues" (p. 4) and persuasion as "any effort to modify an individual's evaluations of people, objects, or issues by the presentation of a message" (p. 25).

The ELM posits that the level of elaboration that an audience devotes to a persuasive message will affect the persuasion process, and therefore, the resulting direction and strength of attitude change. Elaboration has been defined as "the extent to which the person is motivated and/or able to evaluate the central merits of the issue-relevant information presented" (Petty, Kasmer, Haugtvedt, & Cacioppo, 1987, p. 234). In persuasion, elaboration occurs when individuals think about and evaluate issue-relevant information contained in a message. If a person is highly motivated and has the ability to think about issue-relevant arguments, the "elaboration likelihood" is said to be high. If the elaboration likelihood is high, people will attend to a message, access relevant related information from their memories, scrutinize the message arguments in light of the recalled information, draw inferences about the merits of the arguments, and finally form an overall evaluation--or attitude toward--the persuasive appeal (Cacioppo & Petty, 1985).

The ELM suggests two relatively distinct routes of persuasion: the central route, in which elaboration is high and attitude change results from a person's diligent consideration of information the individual considers central to the true merits of a position; and the peripheral route, in which elaboration is low and attitude change occurs because a person makes an inference about the merits of a position based on various simple cues (Petty & Cacioppo, 1981). The route of persuasion influences the amount and persistence of any attitude change that results from a communication.

The ELM helps determine what kinds of persuasion would be most effective in a communication situation depending on the elaboration likelihood. For example, communications that rely on quality of arguments would be effective only in situations where elaboration likelihood is high. If elaboration likelihood is low, communications that stress peripheral cues, such as a celebrity endorser, might be more effective (Petty, Cacioppo, & Schumann, 1983). Interestingly, individuals may end up with the same attitude after a persuasive message regardless of whether it is processed in the central route or the peripheral route. Both types of processing can result in no change in attitudes, change in the direction of the advocated position, change opposite the direction of the advocated position, or change more extreme than the advocated position. Individuals, however, arrive at these positions following very different processes (Petty, Wegener, Rabrigar, Priester, & Cacioppo, 1993).

On any issue, individuals fall on a continuum of elaboration likelihood ranging from no thought about issue-relevant information presented in the arguments to complete elaboration and integration of thoughts into attitude schema (Petty & Cacioppo, 1986a).

As motivation and ability to elaborate on a message increases, peripheral cues become less important in the persuasion process. Conversely, as peripheral cues take on more importance, argument scrutiny becomes less key in persuasion. In short, people are more likely think deeply about information in a message in some contexts, while individuals are more likely to avoid elaboration in other situations.

Moderating Variables

At the heart of the ELM are variables that have been identified as moderating or determining an individual's likelihood of elaborating on a persuasive message. Several factors can affect the route in which an individual processes a communication. Petty and Cacioppo divided these factors into two broad categories: ability and motivation. Under the ELM, an individual must have both the necessary ability and sufficiently high motivation if they are to process a message in the central route. If one or the other is absent, elaboration likelihood is said to be low and peripheral-route processing of information will occur.

Ability variables

Ability factors in the ELM are those that "affect the extent or direction of message scrutiny without the necessary intervention of conscious intent" (Petty & Cacioppo, 1986a, p. 8). Variables that might affect a person's ability to elaborate on a message include message factors, such as whether the message is understandable; situational variables, such as distraction; and individual difference variables, such as topic-relevant prior knowledge. For example, Wood, Kallgren, and Priesler (1985) found that high preexisting knowledge of an topic enables people to process more issue-relevant information than those with low prior knowledge of the subject.

Recently, researchers scrutinizing ability factors have distinguished between ability and opportunity in processing persuasive messages. Opportunity to process is slightly different than ability in that it reflects an external influence on elaboration likelihood, whereas ability is seen as reflecting an internal influence. MacInnis and Jaworski (1989) draw this distinction in defining opportunity as "the extent to which circumstances evidenced during ad exposure are favorable for processing," while defining ability as "skill or proficiency in interpreting . . . information in an ad" (p. 7).

Areni (1991) notes the ramifications of this distinction for advertising research, especially in regard to repetition. Petty and Cacioppo (1986b, see also Cacioppo & Petty, 1985) see repetition of message as enhancing a person's ability to process message arguments: "Repeated presentations of a message provide recipients with a greater opportunity to consider the implications of the content of the message in a relatively objective manner" (p. 143). But Areni argues that this position blurs the line between an individual's internal ability and the external opportunity that repeated exposures gives a person to elaborate on arguments (1991). The same argument could be made for distraction. Petty, Wells, and Brock (1976) found that subjects engaged in a distracting task during a persuasive message had lower ability to think about issue-relevant arguments. Again, this variable was an external, uncontrollable factor for the subjects to deal with, rather than an inherent ability factor that the subjects might be able to control.

Motivational variables

Motivational variables have attracted more attention than ability variables in determining elaboration likelihood, especially among consumer behavior researchers. Petty and Cacioppo (1986) argue that both situational and dispositional factors affect an individuals motivation to attend to and process information. Milburn (1987) has found that situational factors, such as situational activation of different schemas, can alter the typical processing of information. Situational factors affecting a person's motivation to elaborate on a persuasive message include level of involvement with the issue and the number of people besides an individual responsible for message evaluation. Motivation also can be influenced by the persuasion context, for example whether the person has been forewarned of the message's persuasive intent (Petty & Cacioppo, 1986a). Dispositional factors include a person's preexisting intrinsic level of need for cognition.

Need for cognition. Cacioppo and Petty (1982) argued that there are stable--but not invariant--dispositional individual differences in intrinsic motivation to engage in elaboration. Some people enjoy thinking in general and therefore are more likely to form attitudes through central-route processing. Individual differences in what Cacioppo and Petty have termed the "need for cognition" have begun to receive considerably more attention from researchers in the past decade. Need for cognition has been defined as an individual's tendency to engage in and enjoy effortful cognitive endeavors (Cacioppo et al, 1996).[11]

---

[11] Because need for cognition is one of the central independent variables used in this study, this variable will be discussed in greater detail below.

Personal responsibility. Of the situational motivational variables identified to date, personal responsibility probably has received the least attention. This variable, which has been tied to the concept of "social loafing" (see Petty & Cacioppo, 1986b, p. 149), has been operationalized mainly by testing the number of people responsible for evaluating a message. In the seminal study on this variable, Petty, Harkins, and Williams (1980) found that individuals become less motivated to think about message-relevant arguments when they were led to believe that many other people also will be evaluating the message, meaning their personal responsibility for overall message evaluation was low.

Involvement. Personal relevance, or involvement, has by far attracted the most attention from researchers studying elaboration likelihood. The level of involvement is central to the predictions about which routes will be used for processing information. In the model, personal involvement is positively related to the effect that message arguments and evidence have on attitudes. Past research has identified personal involvement as a variable influencing the extent to which issue-relevant arguments will be considered. Consumer behavior and social psychology researchers view a person's involvement with an issue as a moderating variable affecting the level and type of information processing that occurs after persuasive messages (Burnkrant & Sawyer, 1983). As recently as 20 years ago, however, persuasion researchers presumed that greater involvement with an issue was related to greater resistance to change. Individuals highly involved with an issue were thought to discount automatically or negatively evaluate a communication because they were likely to reject a wider range of attitude positions (Eagly & Manis, 1966).

Researchers in the late 1970s began testing the notion that increased involvement is associated with greater information processing. Messages an audience is highly involved with are seen as having greater personal relevance and therefore eliciting more processing that low-involvement messages. For example, one experiment showed that subjects who expected to be asked to debate on an issue could generate more arguments if the issue had high, rather than low, personal relevance (Cialdini, Levy, Herman, Kozlowski, & Petty, 1976). Petty and Cacioppo have similarly used involvement to place individuals on the elaboration likelihood continuum. Petty and Cacioppo (1979) found that increasing involvement with an issue increases a person's motivation to process issue-relevant information and, therefore, could lead either to increased or decreased persuasion, depending on message content. When arguments are compelling for highly involved people, persuasion is enhanced. Conversely, weak arguments decrease persuasion.

Petty, Cacioppo and Goldman (1981) suggest two reasons, one linked to motivation and one linked to ability, why higher involvement might increase the importance of message arguments in persuasion. First, as an issue increases in personal relevance, people become more motivated to exert cognitive energy because they feel greater pressure to hold a reasoned opinion that they could defend later if necessary. Second, more involved people might have greater ability to process issue-relevant arguments because they have better developed schema for thinking about the issue. The ELM posits that different kinds of advertising appeals might work best for different types of audiences. Audiences who are uninvolved with the product or issue would be more likely to use peripheral cues in forming attitudes about the ad. More involved audiences would look for issue-relevant arguments and process in the central route.

Involvement in an issue can be difficult to test in an experiment because of individual differences subjects bring to the setting. For example, an experiment using political involvement as a variable could not simply randomly assign subjects to high- and low-involvement groups because individuals have preexisting levels of interest in politics. However, in other studies, researchers have manipulated involvement. Petty et al. (1983), in testing a disposable razor advertisement, told half the subjects that they would be allowed to select a brand of disposable razor as a gift (high involvement), and the other subjects that they would be able to select a brand of toothpaste (low involvement). To further differentiate between involvement conditions, researchers told the high-involvement group that the advertised product would soon be test marketed locally, while the low-involvement group was told that the product would be test marketed in distant cities.

In another experiment (Petty et al., 1981), involvement was manipulated by telling half of a group of college students that their university was considering requiring a comprehensive exam for graduating seniors the following year (high involvement) and by telling the other half that the change would take place in 10 years (low involvement). Finally, Chaiken (1980) and others have manipulated involvement by telling half the subjects that they would be interviewed after the experiment on the issue they read about (high involvement) and half that they would be asked about an unrelated issue (low involvement).

In sum, for processing to occur in the central route, a person must be not only have the ability and opportunity to process the message but also be involved enough in the issue to be motivated to exert cognitive energy, according to the ELM. If even one of these critical factors is missing, the elaboration likelihood is said to be low, and processing is more likely to occur in the peripheral route.

Peripheral Route Processing

When either ability or motivation to process a message is low, the ELM predicts that an individual will process information in a persuasive communication in the peripheral route. In the peripheral route, attitude change is determined by non-issue-relevant factors, such as the rewards or punishment associated with the message, judgmental distortions in perceiving the message, or inferences drawn about why a position is advocated (Petty & Cacioppo, 1981). Petty and Cacioppo (1986a) have called these "peripheral cues," which refers to "stimuli in the persuasion contest that can affect attitudes without necessitating processing of the message arguments" (p. 18).

Attitude change produced via the peripheral route does not occur because a person has carefully considered the merits of an argument and weighed the pros and cons of an issue. Instead, attitude change stems from the person's reaction to positive or negative persuasion cues associated with the persuasive message. Petty and Cacioppo (1981) have defined persuasion cues as "factors or motives inherent in the persuasion setting that are sufficient to produce the initial attitude change without any active thinking about the attributes of the issue or the object under consideration" (p. 256).

Several theoretical approaches in past persuasion research have been classified as following the peripheral route in the ELM. These approaches stress the following factors: 1) whether a simple inference can be made based on observing one's own behavior; 2) whether the persuasive message falls within one's latitude of acceptance; 3) whether there is a situational use to adopting a particular attitude; 4) whether a stance is linked to issue-irrelevant cues, such as food or pain through classic conditioning (Petty et al., 1983).

Source variables

While primary cues, such as food or pain, received some attention in early persuasion research, secondary cues, especially message source variables, have attracted the most attention in recent years. Secondary cues include source attractiveness, source credibility, and source powerfulness. Much research in the past 15 years has documented source as a variable in persuasive communication effects. Source variables refer to characteristics of the perceived communicator to whom the message is attributed, not the person or organization that actually produced the message, and include demographics such as age, gender, ethnicity, celebrity status and socioeconomic background (McGuire, 1989).

Source attractiveness. Source attractiveness has been identified as a cue that induces processing in the peripheral route. For example, Petty et al. (1983) manipulated the attractiveness of the endorser in a disposable razor advertisement. "Attractive" sources were celebrity athletes, while "unattractive sources" were ordinary citizens from

Bakersfield, Calif. In the low-involvement conditions, source attractiveness significantly affected attitudes toward the product, while the source cue had no impact in the high-involvement condition.

Source liking. Source liking, closely related to source attractiveness, also has been tested as a peripheral route cue. Chaiken (1980) manipulated source liking by having some college students serving as subjects read a message from a source who had insulted their university (un-likable source), while the other subjects were told the communicator had complimented their university (likable source). Attitudes of subjects in the low-consequence conditions were determined primarily by source liking, while the source cue had no significant effect on in the high-consequence conditions.

Source credibility. Of the many source variables that have been tested, source credibility has perhaps attracted the most attention. Perceived source credibility has been identified as a key component in peripheral-route processing. Source credibility studies began with Hovland and his colleagues. For example, Hovland and Weiss (1951) found that communications from sources seen as untrustworthy were viewed as unfair and conclusions drawn from them unjustified. The research demonstrated that when a source was seen as highly "credible," persuasive communication and attitude change could occur (see also Hovland, Janis, & Kelley, 1953).

Source credibility has been conceptualized in many ways. For example, Petty et al. (1981) manipulated source credibility (or expertise) by presenting the same arguments about a senior comprehensive exam to all subjects but telling half that the information came from a report in a local high school newspaper (low expertise), while telling the other half that the information came from a report from the Carnegie Commission on Higher Education, chaired by a Princeton University professor (high expertise). The researchers found that the source credibility manipulation had a stronger effect under the low-personal-involvement condition than under high involvement.

Other researchers also have examined source expertise as in indicator of credibility. Norman (1976) compared source expertise and attractiveness. The attractive source featured in the experiment was a young, good-looking college student, while the expert source was an "unattractive middle-aged man" described as professor of physiological psychology at a large university. While the attractive source was effective in convincing subjects to adopt his opinion regardless of whether he presented any arguments, the expert source was only effective when he presented arguments to support his case, rather than a straight statement of opinion. Several other studies have conceptualized source credibility as trustworthiness, finding that trustworthy sources are more effective in producing attitude change that untrustworthy sources (for example, Hovland & Mandell, 1952).

In the past decade, researchers in mass communication have voraciously studied source credibility as a moderating variable in message effects research. In 1981, Kaid called for more research on how source variables affect political advertising reception. Many have heeded her call. Garramone (1985), using Hovland and Mandell's conceptualization of "trustworthiness" as an indicator of source credibility, found that viewers perceived an independent sponsor as more trustworthy than a candidate sponsor in evaluating political advertising. Garramone and Smith (1984) found that ads from independent sponsors were seen as more trustworthy than ads sponsored by a party or candidate. They also found that ads from an independent sponsor have more effect on candidate image evaluations than ads from "partisan" sources. In addition, Meyer (1988) developed a source credibility index consisting of two factors. The first dealt with believability, based on the assumption that news media need to offer unbiased information; the second dealt with community affiliation, based on news editors' concern that media need to maintain a leadership role in the community.

Message variables

Message variables, which usually are seen as inducing persuasion in the central route, may also serve as peripheral cues under certain conditions. For example, Petty and Cacioppo (1984) tested a low number of arguments (three) against a high number of arguments (nine). Low-involvement subjects were more influenced by the number of arguments, regardless of the quality of the arguments. In contrast, highly involved subjects honed on in argument quality, regardless of the number of arguments presented. The findings suggest that the number of arguments can affect attitudes without issue-relevant thinking.

Central Route Processing

If ability and motivation to process issue-relevant arguments is high, the ELM predicts that an individual will process information in the central route. While peripheral-route processing is based on factors not directly related to the issue in the advocacy, central-route processing deals squarely with the message factors. According to the model, "if a person is motivated and able to think about the message arguments, the following sequence of events will occur: Attention, comprehension, elaboration, integration, then enduring attitude change" (Petty & Cacioppo, 1981, p 265).

Petty et al. (1983) grouped several past theoretical approaches to persuasion as following the central route. These approaches emphasized 1) the cognitive justification of attitude-discrepant behavior; 2) the comprehension, learning, and retention of issue-relevant information; 3) the nature of idiosyncratic cognitive responses to external messages; and 4) the manner in which issue-relevant beliefs are combined into an overall evaluation. In short, any factor dealing with arguments in a message is seen as pertinent in central-route processing. Message factors studied in persuasive communications research have included such variables as delivery style, types of appeals, inclusions and omissions, message organization, message length, and message repetition (McGuire, 1989).

Argument quality

In the ELM, the term arguments refers to "any information contained in a message that permits a person to evaluate the message target (e.g., issue, object, person) along whatever target dimensions are central for that person" (Petty & Cacioppo, 1986a, p. 18). However, the kind of information relevant to evaluating the central merits of an issue varies among situations and among individuals. Individuals will vary in the kinds of information they feel are central to the merits of the position (Petty & Cacioppo, 1986b).

Quality of arguments in favor of a product or issue generally is regarded as the main determinant in the central route to attitude change. In central-route processing, arguments viewed as cogent and compelling will be viewed favorably, resulting in attitude change in the direction of the advocacy. In contrast, weak arguments when processed through the central route virtually always will be resisted. In extreme cases, weak arguments may even cause a boomerang effect, which causes attitude change in the opposite direction of the advocacy (Petty & Cacioppo, 1981).

Experimental manipulation of argument quality allows researchers to tap into the valence of issue-relevant cognitions "to determine under what conditions individuals are thinking about and elaborating on the arguments provided" (Cacioppo, Petty, & Stoltenberg, 1985, p. 224). For example, Petty et al. (1983) manipulated argument quality in a disposable razor ad by giving one group of subjects statements such as "new advanced honing method creates unsurpassed sharpness" (high quality) and the other group statements such as "floats in water with a minimum of rust" (low quality). The researchers found that argument quality only affected attitudes about the razor in the high-involvement group and not in low-involvement subjects. The same results were produced in an earlier study concerning comprehensive exams for graduating university seniors (Petty et al., 1981). High-quality arguments included statistics and data as persuasive evidence (for example, the exams reversed declining scores on standardized achievement tests at other universities). Low-quality arguments were based more on personal opinion and examples (for example, a friend had to take such a test and now had a good job.) The messages were equal in length, and an equal number of arguments was used in each condition.

Other central route variables

In addition to argument quality, a number of other variables have been tested by researchers in conjunction with central-route processing. The number of arguments presented in a persuasive communication has been shown to affect elaboration by providing people with more information to process. Chaiken (1980) gave all subjects cogent arguments; however, half of the subjects received a message containing six strong arguments, while half received a message with only two strong arguments. Attitudes were determined by the number of arguments in the high-consequences conditions only, while number of arguments had no effect in the low-consequences conditions. Source cues also may induce central-route processing. For example, Petty and Cacioppo (1980) found that the physical attractiveness of the endorser could be considered an issue-relevant argument in ads for beauty products.

Attitude change that results from central-route processing tends to be longer-lasting, more resistant to change, and more predictive of future behavior than changes induced via the peripheral route (Cialdini et al., 1981). The enduring nature of central-route processing stems from the fact that information in a message is more likely to have been related to an individual's pre-existing schema that was activated in elaborating on the arguments. The resulting attitude is thought to be more predictive of behavior because relating the information to pre-existing knowledge makes individuals more confident about their attitudes, and in turn, makes them more willing to act on those attitudes. In addition, elaborating on messages gives individuals a stable and accessible attitude, which will be more accessible when they are pressed to act on those attitudes (Cacioppo & Petty, 1985).

Need for Cognition

Voters can be seen as information seekers and processors, looking for information about political issues and candidates and trying to integrate information into their pre-existing attitude and knowledge base. Their ultimate goal, after all, is to try to make an informed choice. To that end, they look to news organizations for help in obtaining, organizing, and prioritizing the facts. But not all voters start with the same knowledge or attitudes, or even with the same motivation to find out and make sense of the political world.

Researchers studying when individuals engage in effortful thinking about issues have examined situational factors, such as involvement in an issue. But some studies using the ELM found that only a portion of the variance between those engaging in different levels of issue-relevant thinking could be explained by situational factors. So researchers began looking for individual differences that could be used to measure chronic variations among people for the need to elaborate on messages. Some individuals have a higher intrinsic motivation to think about topics, including politics. Therefore, these individuals would be more motivated to think critically about a message, regardless of their initial level of involvement with an issue.

To test this individual difference, Cacioppo and Petty developed the "need for cognition," which they argue can play an important part in the persuasion processes.

Before Cacioppo and Petty began researching need for cognition, only one other group of researchers had studied the concept. Cohen, Stotland, and Wolfe (1955) developed a construct called need for cognition, which referred to individuals' need to organize, elaborate on, and evaluate information so they could make sense of the world around them. "Stronger needs lead people to see a situation as ambiguous even if it is relatively structured, indicating that higher standard for cognitive clarity are associated with greater needs for cognition" (Cohen et al., 1955, p. 292). Seeing this construct as having promise as a moderating variable in the ELM, Cacioppo and Petty set out to devise a method of testing this individual difference. Cacioppo and Petty (1982) used Cohen's research as a starting point to devise measure for individual differences in motivation to think deeply about issues, events and people.

To develop a scale, Cacioppo and Petty identified and tested two groups thought to differ in need for cognition: University professors, who were thought to be high in the need for cognition; and factory workers, who served as the low-need-for-cognition group. Out of 45 items thought to be related to need for cognition, 34 discriminated between the two "known" groups. The resulting scale was reliable and showed some convergent and discriminant validity. For example, it tapped a construct distinct from cognitive style, defined as an individual's tendency to think about events piecemeal or in a holistic manner. Factor analysis showed that "much of the inter-individual variation in people's tendency to engage in and enjoy effortful cognitive endeavors could be represented in terms of a single factor, which was called need for cognition" (Cacioppo, Petty, Feinstein, & Jarvis, 1996, p. 197). The researchers envisioned the construct as putting individuals on a continuum from cognitive misers, who hold back from virtually any effortful thinking, to concentrated cognizers, who enjoy problem solving and think deeply about virtually any subject. Cacioppo and Petty cautioned that their definition of the construct is slightly different than Cohen's. While the emphasis in Cohen's conceptualization was on tension reduction, the contemporary use of need for cognition refers to the "statistical tendency of an intrinsic enjoyment individuals derive from engaging in effortful information processing" (Cacioppo, Petty, Kao, & Rodriguez, 1986, p. 1033).

Cacioppo and Petty proposed that individuals high in need for cognition "naturally tend to seek, acquire, think about, and reflect back on information to make sense of stimuli, relationships, and events in their world." In contrast, low-need-for-cognition individuals were characterized as "more likely to rely on others (e.g. celebrities and experts), cognitive heuristics, or social comparison processes to provide this structure" (Cacioppo et al., 1996, p. 198). Need for cognition as defined by Cacioppo and Petty reflected a stable intrinsic motivation in which the process of thinking was stressed over the outcomes of thinking (for example, wanting to make sense of things to bring stability to one's life).

Cacioppo, Petty, and Morris (1983) conducted the first experimental tests of the construct after development of the scale. In two experiments, using two separate issues (requiring senior comprehensive exams and raising student tuition), the researchers found that attitudes of people high in the need for cognition were affected more by argument quality than subjects low in the need for cognition. Checks also revealed that subjects high in the need for cognition reported expending more cognitive energy and recalled messages better regardless of argument quality. Cacioppo et al. (1986) repeated the study

using the issue of student tuition and found similar results. Further analysis showed that

need for cognition was not related to verbal intelligence, and that low-need-for cognition

subjects were acting as "cognitive misers" instead of "verbal dolts." A second part of the

1986 study found a stronger attitude-behavior correspondence between high need for

cognition subjects, at least as measured by behavioral intentions and reported voting

behavior in the 1984 presidential election. More recently, Priester and Petty (1995) found

that attitudes of high-need-for-cognition individuals were influenced by argument quality

regardless of whether they heard information from a "trustworthy" or "untrustworthy"

source. In contrast, those low in the need for cognition scrutinized the message only

when the source was seen as untrustworthy.

Support for the measure's ability to differentiate between types of individuals also

has come from other researchers. A recent review of need for cognition research included

more than 100 studies published in the past 15 years (Cacioppo et al., 1996). Ferguson,

Chung, and Weigold (1985) found that high-need-for-cognition individuals reported

relying more on newspaper and magazines for news than the more passive medium of

television. Ahlering (1987) found that high-need-for-cognition subjects were more likely

to watch the 1984 presidential debates and have more beliefs about the candidates after

the debates. Lassiter, Briggs, and Slaw (1991) found that subjects high in the need for

cognition showed greater explanatory thinking, which in part mediated a person's recall

for a target person's behaviors. Finally, in a study linking need for cognition with interest

in politics, political interaction, political activity, and political media use, Condra (1992) found that individuals high in the need for cognition reported greater interest in the 1988

presidential election, tended to talk about politics more frequently, and had a greater

number of reasons for choosing a particular candidate to support.

Hypotheses

The ELM has several implications for political communications research. Studies

have documented the electorate's declining interest in politics. Given that, the ELM

would predict that most people would give little thought to political messages and

arguments in evaluating candidates. Instead, the majority of voters would rely on

peripheral cues such as source attractiveness (Milburn, 1991). Therefore, election

campaigns are marked with large shifts of opinion (for example, the 1988 and 1992

presidential campaigns), and election issues are relatively short-lived.

Main Effects Hypothesis

This study first asks a general question similar to the experimental adwatch

research described above: Do adwatches change attitudes toward candidates and the

commercials they produce in an election? The main goal of adwatches is to critically

assess the claims a candidate makes in an ad. If a news organization takes a negative stance

on the claims (i.e. points out untruths and misleading ad claims), the expectation would be

that voters also would look at the ad critically. Whether subjects who are exposed to any

type of adwatch, regardless of source and message factors, will view an ad more critically

than those who don't see an adwatch is the central test of the effectiveness of the adwatch

strategy. Therefore, the following two hypotheses were proposed:

H1: Subjects who view a televised ad then read a newspaper adwatch will hold more negative attitudes about the ad than subjects not exposed to an adwatch who view a televised ad and simply reread the text of the ad.

H2: Subjects who view a televised ad then read a newspaper adwatch will hold more negative attitudes about the sponsoring candidate than subjects not exposed to an adwatch who view a televised ad and simply reread the text of the ad.

Individual Differences

This study seeks move beyond examining the main effects of adwatch exposure to build on earlier research. Instead of looking at whether adwatches have general effects on all voters, this study applies ELM to formulate predictions about when and how adwatches affect voters' attitudes. To this end, the study asks a new question: Is the process of attitude change produced by adwatch exposure moderated by variables identified by ELM research?

The ELM suggests that for any subject, some people will process in the central route, relying on issue-based cues, and some people will process in the peripheral route, using more superficial cues. Motivation to pay attention to issues and ability to process issue-oriented messages determine whether people will process in the central route or the peripheral route. One way to examine the motivation of subjects to think about issues is to measure their need for cognition, defined as the degree to which an individual is motivated to structure, integrate, or relate relevant information. Subjects high in the need for cognition like to think about issues and are comfortable thinking deep thoughts. High-need-for-cognition subjects will process adwatch information in the central route, meaning they will use quality of adwatch argument in forming attitudes about the candidates and the ads. Subjects low in the need for cognition look to short-hand cues to help make up their mind,

61

bypassing issue-based arguments. Therefore, low-need-for-cognition subjects should process in the peripheral route and use adwatch source credibility in forming attitudes.

In the study described in the Adwatch Research section above, Cappella and Jamieson (1994) seemed to classify all subjects as low in the need for cognition. "When people are required to make a decision as information comes in (that is 'on line') and exposed to a great deal of complex information relevant to that decision, they are more likely to form an overall attitude on the spot rather than try to remember all the information that goes into that decision" (p. 359).

Adwatch research effects studies to date have failed to examine individual differences among those receiving the messages. Not all voters view and process advertising and adwatches in the same way. Although some studies have shown that adwatches have an impact, current studies have not examined whether adwatches affect some voters more than others and under what conditions adwatches are most likely to affect different types of individuals. Applying the theoretical base of persuasion studies and the Elaboration Likelihood Model is expected to increase understanding of how 1) the quality of the arguments presented in adwatches moderates an adwatch's effectiveness; and 2) the perceived credibility of the news organization publishing an adwatch might change the information's effect on voters.

Adwatch Argument Quality

A review of adwatches prepared in recent elections shows a vast difference in the amount and type of information contained in the reports. The content analysis research examined above shows that some ad coverage is merely descriptive with little analysis.

Adwatches also vary as to whether visual information is discussed, whether analysis of symbols and themes are included, if music is critiqued, and whether the specific ad is placed in context of the overriding theme of the campaign or the strategy of the race, to name a few. For the sake of experimental clarity, this study focuses on one variable in adwatch content--argument quality.

Some arguments are viewed as more substantial than others. For example, a high-quality argument would clarify points and use attribution: "The commercial is untruthful in its claim about the number of government jobs that were reduced while Smith was governor. While 2,000 state jobs were eliminated from the start of his term to the end of his term, these reductions were caused by an early retirement program put in place by his predecessor, according to the state budget office. Smith had nothing to do with the reduction." Low-quality arguments would not go as deeply into an issue or cite established sources: "Smith, like all politicians, overstates his influence on the job cuts. The commercial follows the pattern of exaggerated claims that has marked his campaign." This study seeks to answer the following question: Are high-quality adwatch arguments rebutting claims made in political ads more likely to affect voters attitudes toward a candidate and a political commercial than low-quality adwatch arguments? The following hypotheses were developed to answer this question:

> H3: Subjects who score high on a need for cognition measure who view an ad and then read a high-quality adwatch will hold more negative attitudes toward the ad than high-need-for-cognition subjects who view and ad and then read a low-quality adwatch. Subjects who score low in the need for cognition will be unaffected by argument quality in evaluating the commercial.

H4: Similarly, subjects who score high on a need for cognition measure who view an ad and then read a high-quality adwatch will hold more negative attitudes toward the sponsoring candidate than high-need-for-cognition subjects who view an ad and then read a low-quality adwatch. Again, subjects who score low in the need for cognition will be unaffected by argument quality in evaluating the sponsoring candidate.

Adwatch Source Credibility

Political strategist Roger Ailes, reflecting on the emergence of adwatches during the 1990 races, said most media members producing adwatches tended to pan virtually all ads they reviewed, which cost the media their credibility as objective reviewers.

> This approach was also one of the reasons the 'police force'
> did not have the impact it hoped it would . . . (Journalists)
> are free to write whatever they like, and generally that
> includes their own biases. These newspaper reviews offer
> an opportunity for journalists to voice their own opinion in
> a forum which presents them as 'experts' (Ailes, 1991, p.
> 27).

In effect, the process was nothing more than "journalistic self-gratification," according to Ailes. Although practitioners using adwatches reported mostly positive responses from the public (Wolinsky et al., 1991), voters may have shared Ailes views and discounted adwatch information because they perceived it coming from less-than-credible sources.

To date, no studies have examined how source credibility impacts adwatch effectiveness. In their study of adwatch effects, O'Sullivan and Geiger (1995) touch on that issue in discussing that their demonstrated effects are not surprising, considering that their experiment pitted newspaper articles (an "objective" source) against partisan political ads: "People likely can distinguish between information coming from an ostensibly disinterested source and a persuasive message from a source with a vested interest in the outcome" (p. 11). But the researchers did not experimentally test whether adwatches actually were seen as coming from credible sources and whether this perception affected the influence adwatches had on voter attitudes. This study seeks to test experimentally whether that is the case: Are adwatches from sources perceived as highly credible more likely to affect voters' attitudes toward an advertisement and a candidate than adwatches coming from a source seen as less credible?

Source credibility will be conceptualized in this study by examining perceived objectivity of the adwatch source. Voters would expect a news organization that had consistently attacked a candidate in the past to follow suit in an adwatch, while a news organization that had consistently supported a candidate would be seen as likely to produce an adwatch supporting claims in the candidate's ads. If a news organization consistently supports a candidate on its editorial pages but calls into question the accuracy of his ad claims in a news article, the newspaper should be seen has highly credible because it is breaking from its expected role. In contrast, a news organization that consistently attacks a candidate on its editorial page would be expected to attack the candidate's ad claims in a news article. Therefore, this adwatch source would be seen as less credible. The following hypotheses were suggested to test these assumptions:

H5: Low-need-for-cognition subjects who view an ad and then read an adwatch from a source that has consistently supported the candidate will hold more negative attitudes toward the ad than low-need-for-cognition subjects who view and ad and then read an adwatch from a source that has consistently attacked the candidate. High-need-for-cognition subjects will be unaffected by source credibility.

H6: Low-need-for-cognition subjects who view an ad and then read an adwatch from a source that has consistently supported the candidate will hold more negative attitudes toward the sponsoring candidate than low-need-for-cognition subjects who view and ad and then read an adwatch from a source that has consistently attacked the candidate. High-need-for-cognition subjects again will be unaffected by source credibility.

Research Questions

Condra (1992) studied the effects of need for cognition on a number of related factors, including political interest, political involvement, and political media usage. Eighty-six subjects were tested on an 18-item need for cognition scale, as well as scales measuring political involvement, political activity, and political media use, as well as other items. A series of one-way analyses of variance found subjects high in the need for cognition showed more interest in politics, were more politically involved, and tended to engage in and seek out more political information than the low need for cognition subjects. In their review of more than 100 need for cognition studies, Cacioppo et al. (1996) document several other individual differences thought to be weakly related to need for cognition. However, political interest and involvement were not mentioned. Therefore, this study seeks to replicate Condra's work to test whether need for cognition is related to political interest and activity. Each of the four individual differences hypotheses will be re-tested with political involvement as the moderating variable.

Another research question examined deals with subject's reported voting intentions after viewing an ad and an adwatch. As described above, Ansolabehere and Iyengar (1995) found that voting intention for the candidate critiqued by the adwatch actually increased after exposure to an adwatch. This study will test vote intention as it relates to adwatch exposure. The method used to test these hypotheses and research questions are presented in the next chapter.

CHAPTER III
METHOD

An Overview

In the past two decades, many mass communications researchers have embraced the controlled experiment for testing media effects because it is seen as "the best--and very nearly only--way of finding out what causes what" (Westley, 1981). Therefore, an experimental design was planned and conducted to test the effects of adwatch argument quality and adwatch source bias on attitudes toward political advertisements and their sponsoring candidates. Details of experimental design used to test the hypotheses presented in the previous chapter follow.

Subjects

Subjects were recruited for the experiment from an introductory advertising class at the University of Florida. The researcher spoke to students during their regular class time about a week before the experiment was conducted, inviting students to participate outside of class. Students were given extra credit in exchange for their participation. The total number of students invited to participate was slightly less than 500. Students were invited to participate in one of four sessions. A first group of subjects was tested on one of two dates in February 1996 (Feb. 19 and 20); a second group was tested on one of two dates in March 1996 (March 26 or 27). Analysis of variance on several indicators revealed no significant differences between the groups.[1] Therefore, all subjects were pooled, bringing

the total number of participants in the experiment to 244.

<u>Procedure</u>

When the experimenter invited students to participate in the study, she instructed

them to come to a large classroom that seated about 90 students. She told them that the

study would take about a half hour. As subjects entered, a research assistant told them to

find a seat and wait quietly for the experiment to begin. When all subjects had arrived, the

experimenter told them they were being asked to participate in a study about political

advertising and they would be shown a television commercial.

Each student then handed a nine-page packet. Subjects were instructed to work

through the first five pages, then stop and wait quietly for others to reach that point so they

could all view the television commercial at the same time. The first page informed them of

the general nature of the study, stressed that their participation was voluntary, and asked for

their consent (see Appendix A for the informed consent form). The next three pages asked

basic demographic questions and included measures of general view of newspaper

credibility, need for cognition, and political involvement (details of these measures are

discussed below.) The fifth page gave subjects a brief background about the election for

which the commercial was prepared. A box presenting biographical data on the two

---

[1] Checks were run on several demographic variables, including party identification, gender, ideology, and age. The two groups also were compared on need for cognition, treated here as an independent variable, and on the two evaluation scales served as the dependent variables (see Dependent Variables section below).

68

candidates involved in the race was then presented.[2] At the bottom of page five, the subjects were reminded in writing to stop working and wait quietly for the ad to be shown.

The experimenter then told the subjects that they would view a commercial that one candidate, Jake Godbold, ran in response to attacks made by his opponent, John Delaney. A research assistant turned off the lights, and subjects watched the one-minute commercial on two television sets in the front of the room. After the commercial (discussed below) was broadcast, the experimenter instructed subjects to turn to the next page of their forms, read the newspaper article (discussed in the Manipulation section below) about the commercial they just watched, complete the remainder of the form, and hand the form either to the research assistant or the experimenter on their way out. Dependent measures were included on page seven and eight, and questions testing the manipulations and a note thanking the subjects for their participation in the study were on the last page of the packet.[3]

The Commercial

All subjects were shown the same political advertisement. Before discussing the content of that commercial, it is helpful to discuss the election in which the commercial was originally aired and why it was selected for this study. This research was designed to assess the impact of adwatches by applying the Elaboration Likelihood Model of persuasion. But this work also was designed to extend adwatch research in another area, namely the level of election. All previous experimental adwatch studies have been conducted for adwatches in presidential or statewide contests. No studies have examined adwatches in local elections. This research project aims to fill that void.

_____

[2] Biographies of the candidates, as presented to the subjects, are presented in Appendix B.
[3] Demographic information about the subjects is presented in the following chapter.

A cursory review of adwatches in local newspapers using the news section of the Lexis database found that adwatches in newspapers often examine ads from candidates running for local and state offices. During presidential races, voters are bombarded with news coverage about national candidates, which should--in theory--give them enough information to use their own judgment in analyzing claims made in ads. Voter knowledge of local candidates and issues typically is much lower. Many local elections are non-partisan, leaving voters without the party cue to help them evaluate candidates. Local media, therefore, can play an important role in giving voters the information on which they base their voting decisions in local races. Viewed in this light, adwatches for local races could have more potential to influence voters' views of candidates and the ads than national election adwatches. Therefore their effectiveness should be assessed though research in experiments similar to the current study.

Petty and Cacioppo (1981) argued that that peripheral cues are not likely to be successful in changing attitudes when people have a lot of prior information about an issue or if they are involved in the issue. Therefore, to test need for cognition as a moderating variable in attitude formation and change, an election was chosen in which subjects would have little or no prior knowledge of or involvement with the candidates or issues involved. The commercial selected was from a mayoral contest in Jacksonville, Florida, about 75 miles from the University of Florida, located in Gainesville. It was suspected that few subjects would be familiar with the candidates or the election. Although three Jacksonville television stations are available on Gainesville's cable system, the election had occurred nearly a year before the study was conducted.

The race, which included a high number of attack ads, also was seen as ideal for the study for two additional reasons. First, the two candidates were running for an open seat. Although one candidate, Jake Godbold, had served as the city's mayor in the 1980s, neither candidate was an incumbent in the race. Incumbency has been seen as a powerful factor in elections and among the minds of voters (Jacobson, 1987). Based on the theoretical orientation of this study, incumbency might be seen under the ELM as a peripheral cue. To test for the specific peripheral cue being manipulated in the study, all other information that might serve as a cue, such as incumbency, was held constant. Second, the race was chosen because the city's metropolitan daily news paper, The Florida Times-Union, ran a large number of adwatches on the mayoral election. The newspaper published about two adwatches a week critiquing mayoral race commercials in the six weeks before the election.[4]

The commercial chosen for the experiment was typical of the campaign ads aired during the Delaney-Godbold race and during other local contests. The commercial was produced by the Washington-based Squire/Knapp/Ochs Communications, the same firm that produced Bill Clinton's ads in the 1992 presidential contest. The ad was professionally made and had high production quality, similar to the standards of high-cost spots used on the national level. The commercial as shown to the subjects was on a reel provided directly from the agency, not tapped of the television, and therefore was of excellent visual quality.[5]

---

[4] This information was obtained from the library staff at The Florida Times-Union. The author is grateful to the newspaper's librarians for gathering and copying all adwatches pertaining to the 1995 mayoral race.

[5] The author wishes to thank Shari Yoder and Bill Knapp at Squire/Knapp/Ochs for providing the Godbold commercials and Tom Nolan of Nolan & Associates Advertising Inc. in Bradenton, Florida, for providing commercials from the John Delaney campaign.

The 60-second spot, produced for the Godbold campaign, begins by rebutting being made about Godbold in attack ads produced by the Delaney campaign. A male announcer with a booming voice says, "It's sad. John Delaney's negative attacks distort the facts."[6] The commercial then shows a distorted image of a Delaney campaign ad. The Godbold ad "corrects" Delaney's claim that Godbold added 2,000 bureaucrats during his term as mayor, then goes on the offensive, pointing out "distortions" John Delaney has made in presenting his own record. Ominous music plays in the background as the commercial presents distorted images of Delaney making claims about his background. After each claim, the "correct" version of the facts is written across the screen, superimposed over visuals reinforcing the words,[7] in bold white letters and underlined in red. The announcer also verbally "corrects" the distortion. All of the printed facts are attributed to official sources, such as the Department of Administration and Finance and the State Attorney's Office. The commercial ends with a sinister-looking John Delaney ducking into an office while the announcer says: "John Delaney. First a negative campaign. Now not even telling us the truth about himself."

Jake Godbold does not appear in the ad, except in a small picture at the bottom of the ad in its closing seconds. The picture appears next to small letters stating: "Pd. pol. ad. paid for by the campaign account of Jake Godbold (Dem)." The "(Dem.)" is the only indication in the ad as to which party either candidate belongs to. Political party affiliation is a strong predictor of the way an individual will vote in partisan elections

---

[6] The full text of the ad is included in Appendix C.
[7] For example, while the Godbold ad claims 82 percent of homicide cases were plea bargained under Delaney's tenure as assistant state attorney, the ad presents a visual of a chalk outline of a body on a dark street.

(Campbell, Converse, Miller, & Stokes, 1960). A strong bi-variate correlation has

emerged in past studies between party identification and vote choice (Kessel, 1988).

Therefore, party might also serve as a confounding peripheral cue under the ELM. To

control for party, subjects were not given any information about partisan affiliation in the

biographical information provided on each candidate. It was suspected that because the

subjects were watching a 26-inch television monitor from a distance of at least 10 feet--

and because the "(Dem.)" appeared on the screen for less than five seconds--subjects

would not identify Godbold as the Democrat.[8]

Design

The hypotheses suggested the need for seven experimental groups. Each subject

saw the same commercial then was exposed to one of the following combinations on page

six of their packet: 1) high-quality adwatch arguments from a pro-Godbold newspaper; 2)

low-quality adwatch arguments from a pro-Godbold newspaper; 3) high-quality adwatch

arguments from a pro-Delaney newspaper; 4) low-quality adwatch arguments from a pro-

Delaney paper; 5) high-quality adwatch arguments from a newspaper about which they are

given no information; 6) low-quality adwatch arguments from a newspaper about which

they are given no information; 7) a control in which subjects were not exposed to an

adwatch; instead, each received a printed repetition of the arguments presented in the

commercial. Subjects also were split into high need for cognition and low need for

cognition groups. Therefore, the study used a 2 (high- or low-argument quality) x 3 (pro-

Godbold, pro-Delaney, no source credibility information) x 2 (high or low need for

[8] Results of the test of this assumption are presented in the next chapter.

cognition) between-subjects factorial design. The offset control was divided only into the high and low cognition groups, adding two more cells for a 14-cell design.

To ensure that the manipulated conditions in an experiment are exclusively responsible for the differences among groups, the groups receiving the varied treatments must be equal prior to the experiment. To be able to infer treatment-caused change in this study, random assignment to treatment groups was employed. Using randomization in an experiment is vital to equate experimental and control groups or the several treatment groups (Campbell & Stanley, 1968). Randomization can rule out some of the most dangerous threats to internal validity, including selection, selection-maturation, and regression. It also creates the conditions for which the most common statistical models were designed. However, Cook and Campbell (1979) warn: "While randomization is the best single means of increasing our confidence in causal inferences, it is not a panacea" (p. 86). Despite some of the limitations, random assignment to groups was viewed as the best available method of testing the hypotheses in this study. Therefore, the seven different forms, each representing a group, were stacked in random order using a random numbers table. At the time of the experiment, the researcher and an assistant handed the forms down the rows in which students were seated.

Independent Variables

To test hypotheses using the Elaboration Likelihood Model, studies must have at least three independent variables: a manipulation of issue-relevant argument quality; a manipulation of a peripheral cue, usually a source variable; and a third variable that would trigger subjects to process in either the central or peripheral route. This study uses three independent variables to test the hypotheses. The first two, argument quality and source bias, are experimentally manipulated variables; the third, need for cognition, is a dispositional, pre-existing inclination in individuals that cannot be manipulated.

Manipulation of Argument Quality

High- and low-quality adwatch arguments were devised by the researcher after a review of dozens of adwatches in local newspapers throughout the country. Most adwatches address between two and four claims made by an ad. The adwatches in this study addressed three statements made by the targeted. The high-quality arguments attacked those ad claims directly by addressing the issue and providing facts to refute claims made in the ad. Low-quality arguments rebutting the three statements did not directly address the claims. This study was designed so that approximately half of the subjects would receive high-quality arguments and half of the subjects would receive low-quality arguments.[9]

Petty and Cacioppo (1981, 1986) note that while there will always be some differences in the quality individuals ascribe to the same argument, the key to testing hypotheses with the ELM is to develop arguments that the majority of a specified population finds either compelling or weak. To achieve this goal, the researchers suggest several steps in developing arguments. This study followed those steps in generating "strong" and "weak" arguments to be used in the adwatches.

---

[9] The number would be slightly less than half of the total subject pool because of the use of the off-set control group, in which 1/7 of the subjects would receive no argument quality or source bias manipulations.

Pilot-testing arguments

First, the researcher identified three statements or claims in the John Delaney

commercial that an adwatch might critique. Then six to eight arguments rebutting each of

those statements were generated that the researcher intuitively viewed as either strong or

weak. In a pilot test of argument quality, subjects similar to those who would be tested

during the experiment were asked to rate the arguments. Subjects were given brief

background on the election and told that they were helping the Delaney campaign come up

with the best responses to Jake Godbold's attacks. After each statement, the subjects were

asked to evaluate the quality of a list of responses on a four-item semantic differential scale.

Semantic differentials have been used to assess attitudes since Osgood (1965) suggested

that researchers could measure attitudes by having people rate an object on bipolar adjective

pairs that represented the extreme of a continuum of feelings. To measure the quality of

arguments, subjects were asked to rate the responses (on a seven-point scale[10]) on four

dimensions: Weak/Strong; Unconvincing/Convincing; Irrational/Rational; Not

believable/Believable.[11]

Twenty-five subjects participated in the argument-rating test. The median age was

22, and all but four were under age 26. Nineteen said they were currently taking college

[10] Subjects were instructed that numbers 1 and 7, each closest to one of the words in the
adjective pair, represented a very strong feeling one way or the other; numbers 2 and 6
indicated strong feelings; numbers 3 and 5 indicated fairly weak feelings; and number 4
represented an undecided view of the dimension.
[11] Petty & Cacioppo (1986b) suggest testing for believability with another panel of
subjects after the first panel has rated persuasiveness: "Our goal is to develop arguments
that are strong and weak, but that do not strain credulity: (p. 134). Because the researcher
had a limited amount of subjects, these two dimensions were tested at the same time.

classes. Subjects in the pilot study were split evenly on party identification. Eight subjects identified themselves as Democrats, 8 as Republicans, 7 as independent, and 2 as "other."

The mean score for each response was calculated by averaging responses on four dimensions used to rate each argument. The arguments were then ranked weakest to strongest by mean score. Means for the responses to the first set of arguments ranged from 3.24 to 4.46; means for the second set of arguments ranged from 3.81 to 4.82; means for the third set of responses ranged from 3.01 to 4.86. To assess whether the strongest and weakest arguments were significantly different from other arguments, paired t-tests were conducted. The strongest and weakest arguments rebutting the first ad claim differed significantly (t (24) = 3.20, p = .004); as did the those refuting the third ad claim (t (24) = - 5.50, p <.001). For the responses to the second ad claim, the two "weakest" arguments were virtually identical in mean and standard deviation, and each was significantly different from the strongest argument (t (24) = 2.54, p = .018 for the argument with the lowest mean; and t (24) = -2.56, p = .017 for the argument with the next to lowest mean).

Argument selection

Once the pilot study produced arguments that varied significantly in their perceived strength, the statements were checked for factors that could confound the argument quality manipulation. For example, studies have found that length of arguments--like number of arguments--can be used as a peripheral cue. Subjects exposed to longer arguments see them as more persuasive than shorter arguments (Petty & Cacioppo, 1986b). In addition, "objective" facts and figures used in an argument could serve as a peripheral cue. Subjects might see data as more "official" and therefore more persuasive than arguments that do not contain numbers.

With those considerations in mind, arguments were selected that were equal in length and in the use of numbers for both the high- and low-argument-quality treatments. For the first and third ad claims, the refuting arguments that tested "strongest" (the highest means on the four-item persuasiveness scale) and "weakest" (the lowest means) met these conditions. For the second ad claim, the strongest argument was used in contrast with the second-weakest argument, which was significantly different from the strongest argument (see previous section). The second-weakest argument was selected for use in the study primarily to balance the statements for length and use of numbers. It also was thought that the argument that tested weakest, while not statistically significantly different from the next weakest argument, might make subjects question whether the adwatch they were reading came from an actual newspaper, therefore compromising the external validity of the study.[12] This selection left the following arguments to counter statements made in the commercial:

Ad Claim 1: John Delaney says he wants to reduce government spending. But as Jacksonville's general counsel, John Delaney increased his own budget by $1.4 million.

Adwatch high-quality argument: "The $1.4 million increase in the general counsel's budget represented a 3.5 percent increase. During the same period, the budgets of other city departments increased an average of 7.9 percent, indicating that Delaney held costs in check better than other officials."

---

[12] The argument that was rejected was refuting a statement about the rate of plea Bargains John Delaney was involved in making. It argued "Criminals prefer plea bargains because they usually get lighter sentences than if they went to trial."

Adwatch low-quality argument: "While Delaney did increase the general counsel's budget by $1.4 million, the department's budget is such a small amount of the entire city budget that increases don't really register on Jacksonville's finances."

Ad Claim 2: While John Delaney was Florida's assistant state attorney, 82 percent of homicide cases were plea bargained.

Adwatch high-quality argument: "The percentage quoted in the ad for the plea bargains is correct. But the national average for plea bargains is 91 percent; Florida's 82 percent is the third lowest in the nation."

Adwatch low-quality argument: "The percentage quoted in the ad is correct. But more than 75 percent of the decisions about plea bargains were made by the state attorney; the assistant state attorney has little say in plea bargains."

Ad claim 3: Delaney has accepted 25 pay raises, and his $120,000 salary as general counsel is more than even the mayor makes.

Adwatch high-quality argument: "Delaney's $120,000 salary is consistent with what general counsels for other cities the same size as Jacksonville are paid."

Adwatch low-quality argument: "Delaney did accept 25 pay raises. But while Delaney is paid more than the mayor, he is paid $10,000 less than the governor of Florida." [13]

---

[13] The pilot test of argument quality measured argument quality differences in a within-subject design. Because the experiment used a between-subjects design, a manipulation check was included in the study to test whether the subjects saw high- and low-quality arguments as significantly different was included in the questionnaire used during the experiments. These results are presented in the next chapter.

<u>Adwatch presentation</u>

The arguments were placed in an adwatch format similar to that used in many newspapers. The researcher, who has newspaper layout and design experience, created the top half of a page from the <u>Jacksonville Gazette</u>.[14] The page, which included an adwatch and three non-related news stories, looked like it came from an actual newspaper. The adwatch was boxed and placed in the upper left corner of the "newspaper" page. The other articles on the page were only partially shown to the subjects, as if a section of the newspaper page featuring the adwatch had been cut out for them to review. (See Appendix D for the high- and low-quality adwatches developed for this study. The actual adwatch that <u>The Florida Times-Union</u> used to critique this particular campaign ad is in Appendix E.) The adwatch was titled "Political Ad Check," the same title given to actual adwatches in <u>The Florida Times-Union</u>. Following a byline, facts about the commercial--including candidate sponsoring the ad, the election, ad length, media used, and date aired--were listed. A section titled "What it says" restated claims made in the ad. Finally a section titled "What's the truth?"[15] listed either all high-quality or all low-quality arguments, depending on the treatment condition. When completed, both the high-quality adwatch and the low-quality adwatch took up 17 lines of type. The high-quality adwatch contained six numbers; the low-quality contained four.

All seven experimental conditions contained a repetition of the "facts" stated in the commercial. The six groups that read an adwatch all received a newspaper repetition

---

[14] A fictional newspaper was created to avoid any pre-existing opinions about <u>The Florida Times-Union</u> from confounding the independent variable manipulations, especially the source credibility manipulation.

[15] Again, these are the same as the sections headings used by <u>The Florida Times-Union</u>.

of the statements in the ad; the control group was given the text of the ad in printed form to read. This was done to ensure that repetition of the ad was equal across conditions and, therefore, would not confound attitude toward the message. Cacioppo and Petty (1979) found that while repetition of a message had no impact on recall, agreement with a message first increased then decreased as exposure frequency increased.

Manipulation of Source Credibility

Source credibility was operationalized in this study by manipulating the perceived objectivity of the source. According to the ELM, a non-credible source could cause subjects processing in the peripheral route to reject the advocacy. Other research has linked manipulating source objectivity to source credibility. Bias was identified by Meyer (1988) as one of two factors in credibility. Meyer called this factor, which was based on the assumption that news media need to offer unbiased information, believability. Garramone and Smith's (1984) concept of "trustworthiness," which they identified as one dimension of source credibility, is closely linked to source objectivity and believability.

Newspaper objectivity was chosen as the peripheral cue manipulation in this study because of the real-world use of adwatches. Whereas Petty et al. (1981) used a high school newspaper as a non-credible source and a report from a Princeton University professor as a highly credible source, that type of manipulation is not applicable to adwatches. Adwatches appear only in the news media. Making the distinction between a highly credible metropolitan newspaper and a non-credible metropolitan newspaper might strain credulity. In contrast, subjects could reasonably believe that a newspaper overtly favors one candidate or the other, especially in light of anti-media backlash that emerged in the

1990s and the "media bias" issues raised in the 1992 and 1994 elections.

Therefore, credibility of adwatch source was manipulated by altering a statement

presented to subjects before reading the adwatch. At the top of the page on which the

newspaper adwatch appeared--outside the "newspaper" page created for the experiment--a

section called "Newspaper Objectivity" appeared. The design included three treatment

groups for source credibility: a newspaper strongly in favor of Jake Godbold (pro-

Godbold); a newspaper strongly opposed to Godbold (anti-Godbold); and no newspaper

objectivity information.[16] Subjects receiving a newspaper objectivity manipulation read

one of the following messages:

> Pro-Godbold newspaper: "This newspaper, the Jacksonville Gazette, wrote
> editorials endorsing Jake Godbold during both of his previous campaigns for mayor.
> When Godbold was mayor, the newspaper's editorial page agreed with his stance on
> issues more than 90 percent of the time. The publisher of the paper is good friends
> with Godbold and has contributed money to the Godbold campaign."

> Anti-Godbold newspaper: "This newspaper, the Jacksonville Gazette, wrote
> editorials attacking Jake Godbold and endorsing his opponents during both of
> Godbold's previous elections. When Godbold was mayor, the newspaper's editorial
> page opposed his stance on issues more than 90 percent of the time. The publisher
> of the paper has a long-running feud with Godbold and has contributed money to
> candidates running against Godbold."[17]

---

[16] The no newspaper objectivity group was used as a baseline measure for this variable
and was not included in the hypotheses for source credibility. A description of how this
group was treated in data analysis is presented in the next chapter. The 35 subjects in the
offset control group also did not receive any newspaper objectivity information.
[17] A manipulation check testing whether the subjects in the experiment viewed these
statements as indicating the newspaper was biased (either pro-Godbold or anti-Godbold)
was included in the questionnaire used during the experiment. The results are presented
in the next chapter.

Need for Cognition

The third experimental variable, need for cognition, has been shown to determine

the route in which subjects process information. Subjects high in the need for cognition

should process adwatch information in the central route, whereas subjects low in the need

for cognition should process adwatch information in the peripheral route. To assess the

degree to which individuals tend to engage in elaborative thought, Cacioppo and Petty

(1982) developed the Need for Cognition Scale (NCS). The scale as first developed

included 34 items, which used a 9-point Likert-type scale (-4 to +4). The resulting scale

was distinguished by one dominant factor, which explained 27 percent of the variance.[18]

The NCS also was reliable, with a maximized Cronbach's alpha coefficient of .91. Osberg

(1988) tested the convergent and discriminant validity of the NCS by examining the

relationships between need for cognition and several personality dimensions. The findings

supported the construct validity of Cacioppo and Petty's scale, for example finding that

scores were positively associated with measures of self-esteem but unrelated to measures of

sociability and loneliness.

Recognizing that a 34-item scale might be hard to administer in some situations,

Cacioppo, Petty, and Kao (1984) developed an "efficient assessment' of need for cognition.

By selecting items on the 34-item NCS with the highest factor loadings and calculating

Cronbach's alpha as each successive item was added, the researchers developed an 18-item

---

[18] One study re-tested the 34-item scale with what the authors termed "appropriate
methods for the factor analysis of dichotomous variables" and found three separate
factors: Cognitive persistence, cognitive confidence, and cognitive complexity (Tanka,
Panter, & Winborne, 1988, p. 35). However, most NCS studies since have supported
Cacioppo and Petty's finding of one dominant factor.

NCS. The shortened NCS also had one dominant factor, which explained 37 percent of the variance, and was highly reliable (Cronbach's alpha = .90). In addition to having high internal consistency and substantial validity, the scale high test-retest reliability (r = .88, p < .0001), which indicated that need for cognition is a highly stable individual difference variable (Sadowski & Gulgoz, 1992).

At the same time that Cacioppo and Petty were developing a shorter version of the NCS, other researchers were tackling the same problem. For example, Dutch researchers have consistently used a shortened, 15-item version of the NCS (see review by Cacioppo et al, 1996). In addition, Perri and Wolfgang (1988), reasoning that because the original 34-item was unidimensional a shorter version would be as well, selected 16 of the 34 items based on the highest factor loadings from the scale.[19] The resulting scale yielded one factor, which accounted for 38.8 percent of the variance and was highly reliable, with a coefficient alpha of .88.

Another shortened version of the NCS that has been used was created by Ferguson et al. (1985) after pre-tests showed that the 34-item scale was unwieldy in survey research. The researchers selected 15 statements from Cacioppo and Petty's original scale based on statistical significance, reliability estimates, salient factor loadings and ease of comprehension by subjects.[20] In addition, Ferguson et al. replaced the nine-point Likert-type scale to a seven-point response scale. Finally, to reduce response bias, the researchers

---

[19] Perri and Wolfgang's 16-item scale used 10 of the same items used in Cacioppo and Petty's shortened 18-point NCS.

[20] Ferguson et al.'s 15-items scale contained 13 of the 18 items used in Cacioppo and Petty's efficient assessment of need for cognition. However, the two items used in the Ferguson et al. scale that do not appear in the 18-item scale also appear in the Perri and Wolfgang scale (see Perri & Wolfgang, Table 2, p. 957).

positively worded some items and negatively worded others. In data analysis, responses to negatively worded items were recoded. The scale produced was highly reliable, with a Cronbach's alpha of .86.

The Ferguson et al. scale was used to assess need for cognition in this study for several reasons. First, the 15-item scale is virtually identical to the Cacioppo et al's 18-item NCS. Because of the length of several other measures on the questionnaire, a shorter scale, even a few lines shorter, was desired if available. Ferguson's scale also was nearly as equally reliable. Finally, Ferguson's reliability analysis tested the scale with a seven-point Likert-type response measure, which was desired in this study, as opposed to the nine-point response measure used in the NCS as developed by Cacioppo et al. (1984).

Therefore, need for cognition was measured in this study by asking individuals to respond to the following 15 statements:

1. I like tasks that require little thought once I've learned them.*

2. I prefer to think about small daily projects instead of long-term projects.*

3. I really enjoy a task that involves coming up with new solutions and problems.

4. I don't like to have the responsibility of handling situations that require a lot of thinking.*

5. The idea of relying on thought to make my way to the top does not appeal to me.*

6. I prefer complex problems to simple problems.

7. I think only as hard as I have to.*

8. I prefer to just let things happen rather than trying to understand why they turned out that way.*

9. The notion of thinking abstractly is not appealing to me.*

10. I would rather do something that requires little thought than something that is sure to challenge my thinking abilities.*

11. Thinking is not my idea of fun.*

12. I find satisfaction in deliberating hard and for long hours.

13. I prefer my life to be filled with puzzles that I must solve.

14. Simply knowing the answer rather than understanding the reasons for the answer to a problem is fine with me.*

15. I try to anticipate and avoid situations where there is a likely chance that I will have to think in depth about something.*[21]

Respondents' scores for each of the 15 self-appraisal items were summed and averaged to create an index. Specifically, the respondent's need for cognition was based on numerical scores from 1 to 7, in which 1 meant that the subject "very strongly disagreed" with the statement and 7 meant the subject "very strongly disagreed." Four ("neither agree nor disagree") was the neutral point.

<u>Political Involvement</u>

A scale measuring political involvement was included to test the research questions pertaining to the link between need-for-cognition and political activity and interest. The scale, developed for this project, was compiled by reviewing dozens of political

---

[21] Items with an * were reverse coded.

participation measures used in past studies. Eleven items were chosen based on the past

success of these items in measuring political involvement. Items also were selected that

would best fit the real-world experience of the subject pool, many of whom only recently

had become old enough to vote. Subjects were asked to check the box that best describes

how often they participated in the political action described.[22] The eleven items selected are

as follows:

1. Talk with my friends or family about politics.

2. Vote in elections in which I am an eligible voter.

3. Work for a campaign by doing things like distributing information or making phone calls.

4. Contribute money to a candidate's campaign.

5. Wear a button or put a bumper sticker on my car showing my support of a candidate.

6. Write a lawmaker to express my views on an issue.

7. Watch television news about politics.

8. Watch political debates.

9. Read a political stories in a newspaper or magazine.

10. Attend political rallies or events.

11. Pay attention to political advertising on TV

A high number on the scale would indicate that the person was interested in politics,

while a lower number indicated disinterest in politics. The first six items on the scale were

---

[22] The answers were coded as follows: 1 = Never; 2 = Rarely; 3 = Sometimes; 4 = Often, 5 = Always.

designed to tap into political action, while the last five items were linked to communicating about politics.

Dependent Variables

Scores of variables have been used to measure subject response to advertising stimuli. For example, researchers have measured individuals' perceptions of source credibility, liking, familiarity, confusion, empathy, relevant information, and other variables related to advertising. Evaluation measures for political advertising are a bit more limited. Traditionally, political advertising studies typically have evaluated three variables: evaluation of an ad or series of ads, evaluation of the candidate sponsoring a commercial, and evaluation of the candidate being attacked in a commercial (Garramone & Smith, 1984; Roddy & Garramone, 1988; Pinkleton, 1993; Tinkham & Weaver-Lariscy, 1994). Because adwatches are aimed at affecting voters' perception of an ad and its sponsoring candidate, this study uses commercial evaluation and sponsoring candidate evaluation as the dependent measures.

Commercial Evaluation

Political commercials have been evaluated in a number of ways. Garramone and Smith (1984) asked subjects to rank a commercial on six attributes--believable, fair, annoying, convincing, tasteful, and informative--using a scale of 1 for "not at all" to 7 for "very." However, most research has evaluated commercials with semantic differentials, which are adjective pairs representing extreme ends of a spectrum of feelings. In addition, several different attributes of campaign ads have been tested. Tinkham and Weaver-Lariscy

(1994) used items that tapped the attributes of confusion, entertainment, relevant news, empathy, familiarity, and alienation. Pinkleton (1993) identified six attributes as considered important to both political advertising and comparative product advertising success: believable, unbiased, informative, interesting, fair, and useful. Roddy and Garramone (1988) used items measuring how informative, believable, and persuasive the political commercial was.

Because journalists developed adwatches to help voters decide what to believe or not to believe in political advertising, this study focuses on believability. One scale designed to tap this attribute was a 10-item television advertising believability scale developed by Beltramini (1982, also see Beltramini, 1988). The scale consists of 10 semantic differentials each operationalized using a five-place response scale format. Scores are derived by averaging responses on the 10 items, such that higher scores reflect greater believability. Scores for the scale have ranged from 3.54 to 6.28 in previous studies. Reliability of the scale has been measured as high as .95, with inter-item correlations as high as .69. Thorson, Christ, and Caywood (1991) used a similar "ad attitude" scale in evaluating issue/image strategies in political commercials. This scale also has been shown to be highly reliable (Cronbach's alpha = .87).

Because many of the items in the two scales were similar, this study uses a combination of the two. The items that most directly measured the constructs of believability and credibility were used. Therefore, the commercial evaluation scale used in this study consisted of the following 10 items: Unbelievable/Believable; Untrustworthy/Trustworthy; Not convincing/Convincing; Not credible/Credible;

Unreasonable/Reasonable; Deceptive/Truthful; Questionable/Unquestionable;

Inconclusive/Conclusive; Unethical/Ethical; and Inaccurate/Accurate.

The adjective pairs were placed on either end of a row of seven boxes. Subjects

were instructed to check one box out of seven on each line that best described their feeling

toward the ad they just saw. The numbers 1 and 7 were placed nearest to the words and

represented "very strong feelings." Boxes 2 and 6 were used to represent "strong feelings";

boxes 3 and 5 represented "fairly weak feelings"; and box "4 indicated an undecided

response.

Sponsoring Candidate Evaluation

Attitude toward the candidate also has been measured extensively using bi-polar

adjective pairs as anchors. Attributes that have been seen as useful in previous studies

investigating the impact of political advertising on candidate evaluation have included

intelligence, sincerity, believability, honesty, persuasiveness, concern, qualifications, ethical

standing, and trustworthiness. Because adwatches are designed to affect voters' perception

of each of these attributes, many of them were included in a candidate evaluation measure

developed for this study.

This research used bi-polar adjective pairs taken from both Garramone (1985) and

Thorson et al. (1991). Garramone's measure was developed to test the perceptions of the

target of the political advertisement, namely the opponent of the sponsoring candidate.

However, adwatches transform an ad's sponsoring candidate into the "target" by creating a

persuasive message attacking ad claims. Garramone used a nine-item measure, which

produced Cronbach's alpha of .82. Thorson et al. used a 19-item scale, which used six of

Garramone's items and 13 additional items. That measure also had strong reliability with

Cronbach's alpha .94. After examining those two measures, the following scale was

created for the current study: Incompetent/Competent; Weak/Strong; Dumb/Smart;

Unqualified/Qualified; Cannot be trusted/Can be trusted; Unsympathetic/Sympathetic;

Unfriendly/Friendly; Irrational/Rational; Unappealing/Appealing;

Inexperienced/Experienced[23]

Voting Intention

One of the research questions in this study required a measure of voting intention.

After viewing the commercial and reading the adwatch, subjects were asked: "If the election

were held tomorrow and you were eligible to vote, which statement best describes how you

would vote? Subjects were asked to select from "Would definitely vote for John Delaney";

"Would probably vote for John Delaney"; "Still undecided: Support John Delaney and Jake

Godbold equally"; "Would probably vote for Jake Godbold"; "Would definitely vote for

Jake Godbold"; and "I would not vote in this election."[24]

Path for Analysis

The next chapter begins with an examination of the descriptive statistics of the data

set. Then an analysis of the manipulation checks used in this study will be presented.

Factor analyses and reliabilities of the scales will be examined, as well as tests of the

---

[23] As with the commercial evaluation measure, respondents were asked to check one box on each line (numbered from 1 to 7) that best described how they felt toward the sponsoring candidate.

[24] These choices were only given to the 123 subjects who participated in the experiment in March. The 121 subjects who participated in February were given a forced choice measure: "If the election were held tomorrow, who would you vote for?" and asked to check either John Delaney or Jake Godbold. This was done for future research examining how forced vote measures vary from other methods of measuring vote intention.

assumptions made in designing this study. The hypotheses will be tested using experimental Analysis of Variance (ANOVA). Finally, results of the research questions will be presented.

CHAPTER IV
RESULTS

Analysis of variance (ANOVA) was used to test effects of need for cognition, adwatch argument quality, and newspaper credibility on evaluations of the ad and the candidate sponsoring the ad. Analysis of variance is a statistical test used to test the difference in means between two or more groups. It is especially valuable in identifying the effects of a treatment or manipulation on the degree to which cases manifest a concept (Manheim & Rich, 1991).

The chapter begins with a descriptive analysis of the sample on demographic data, political views and need for cognition. Next, the properties of the scales used as measures for both independent and dependent measures are discussed. Results of the manipulation checks and the tests of the assumptions made are then presented. Finally, tests of the hypotheses are discussed.

Descriptive Analysis

Demographic Data

During the four experimental sessions, 244 subjects participated in the study. Of those, 55 percent (n = 135) were female and 45 percent (n = 109) were male. Subjects ranged in age from 18 to 33 (M = 20.9, SD = 1.87). Fifty-nine of the subjects were advertising majors, 58 were majoring in other fields in the College of Journalism and Communications (public relations, journalism, and telecommunications), and 127 had majors outside the journalism college. Two hundred of the subjects reported that they were

registered to vote, while 43 said they were not registered voters.[1]

Political Views

When asked to describe their political views, nine reported being very liberal, 36

said they were liberal, 56 called themselves moderate liberals, 64 said they were "middle-

of-the-road," 47 said they were moderate conservatives, 26 classified themselves as

conservative, and three reported being very conservative.[2] Political leanings also were

measured by asking subjects the party for which party they most often vote. One hundred

and seven identified themselves as Democrats, 97 as Republicans, 20 as independents, and

seven as "other."[3]

Need for Cognition

Subjects' classification as being high or low in the need for cognition was based on

their Need for Cognition Scale (NCS) scores. Researchers have been divided on how to

split need for cognition scores for analysis. Cacioppo et al. (1983) split the scores on the

scale into high, medium, and low need for cognition. Subjects were ranked based on their

scores on the NCS, and only those in the upper or lower thirds were retained for analysis.

The middle third of the scores were discarded. The researchers explained this choice:

> The data from subject whose scores on the NCS fell near the
> median were not analyzed in the initial tests of the
> hypothesis because post hoc analyses of the pilot studied
> suggested that subjects from a homogenous population (e.g.,
> from introductory psychology classes) whose NCS scores
> fell near the median responded to a variety of experimental
> tasks in a similar fashion whether their score was marginally

---

[1] One subject left this response blank.
[2] Three subjects did not answer this item.
[3] Thirteen subjects left this item blank.

above or below the median. It was assumed a prori that by deleting the data from these subjects in the present study, the responses to the persuasive communication attributable to need for cognition would be more apparent (Cacioppo et al., 1983, note 4, p. 811).

Lassiter et al. (1991) also used a three-way split, omitting the middle group from data analysis and testing only the extreme scorers. In contrast, Ahlering (1987) and Condra (1992) used a median split to divide subjects into low- and high-need-for-cognition groups, retaining all scores in their data analysis. Cacioppo et al. (1986) also shifted to using a median split for the variable.

This study, while recognizing the validity of the arguments made by Cacioppo et al. (1983) for a three-way split for need for cognition scores, uses a median split for initial hypothesis testing. This choice was based on past research that tested the NCS with both a median split and a three-way split with the same subject pool. In previous studies (for example Cacioppo et al., 1983), virtually no differences emerged in the patterns and directions of the findings and few differences were found in levels of significance. Therefore, subjects in this study were ranked on need for cognition scores then divided at the median, with those falling below the median classified as low in the need for cognition. Subjects with scores above the median were classified as high in the need for cognition. As a check, however, reanalyzes of all hypotheses also were conducted using only scores in the top and bottom third of the need for cognition scale. No differences in direction or significance of findings were reported with an extreme-scores split.

As described in the previous chapter, the need for cognition scale used in this study included 15 items, each of which could be answered from 1 (a low need for cognition response) to 7 (a high need for cognition response). Average scores on the 15-item need for cognition scale ranged from 2.60 to 6.67. The mean score was 4.81, the median was 4.87, and the mode was 5.13. For the median split, those scoring below 4.87 were classified as low in the need for cognition, while those scoring at 4.87 and above were classified as high in the need for cognition. The split resulted in 117 low-need-for-cognition subjects, a group that was tightly distributed around its mean (M = 4.24, SD = .49). The mean score for the low-need-for-cognition subjects was significantly different from the mean of the 127-high-need-for-cognition subjects (M = 5.34, SD = .37).[4] The tight distribution around the two significantly different means indicates a strong median split for the scores. The need for cognition along with the random assignment to groups produced cell sizes from 13 to 19.

The Scales

This study relied primarily on three scales for the initial tests of hypotheses. One, the Need for Cognition Scale (NCS), measured the independent variable. Two scales, an advertising believability measure and a candidate evaluation measure, were used to gauge dependent measures. As discussed in Chapter III, the scales all had proven highly reliable in previous research. In addition, each scale typically produced one dominant factor that explained a large percentage of the variance.

Scale properties in this study were examined through two methods. First, each scale was examined using a principal components factor analysis. A factor analysis asks the degree to which clusters of inter-correlated variables may represent fewer underlying, more

---

[4] This uneven split was caused by a cluster of 13 scores at 4.87. The exact median was 4.867. If the scores at 4.87 were included with the low need for cognition group instead, the split would have been more unequal (130 low scores and 114 high scores).

basic, hypothetical variables (Williams, 1986). Principal factor analysis for each scale typically showed one dominant factor, negating the need for analysis of a rotated factor matrix. In addition, the internal consistency of the scales was analyzed using a reliability analysis, in which Cronbach's alpha and average inter-item correlation coefficient were examined. Findings in this study measuring scale properties closely replicate findings from previous research using the three scales, in which the scales each produce only one factor and are highly reliable. Results for each scale are discussed briefly.

The Need for Cognition Scale

Principal factor analysis of the 15-item Need for Cognition Scale (NCS) using standard principal components analysis resulted in four factors with Eigenvalues greater than 1.0. However, several of the items loaded on more than one factor, and all items loaded above .39 on the first factor, suggesting a one-factor solution. The first factor was clearly dominant, with an Eigenvalue of 4.9. This dominant factor explained 32.6 percent of the variance. The other three factors that emerged explained a much smaller portion of the variance: The second factor (Eigenvalue = 1.3) explained 9.2 percent of the variance; the third factor (Eigenvalue = 1.1) explained 7.4 percent; the third factor (Eigenvalue = 1.0) explained 6.8 percent. Finally, an examination of scree plots also suggested a one-factor solution for the NCS.

Most past studies using the NCS have reported one dominant factor with several smaller factors with Eigenvalues just greater than 1.0 (see Cacioppo et al., 1996, for a review factor analyses reported in previous research). Because of the dominance of the first factor, most researchers have analyzed the NCS as a single measure. This research follows suit, combining all 15 items into a single index. Reliability analysis of the scale supports

this decision. Cronbach's alpha (Cronbach, 1951) for the 15-item measure in this study was

.84 and would have decreased if any single item was deleted. In addition, the average inter-

item correlation coefficient for the scale was .27.

Advertising Believability Scale

Principal factor analysis of the 10-item commercial evaluation scale produced two

factors with Eigenvalues greater than 1.0. Seven factors clearly loaded on the first factor.

The remaining three items loaded on both factors but always more strongly on the first

factor. The first factor (Eigenvalue = 5.1) was clearly dominant, explaining 51.1 percent of

the variance. The second factor had an Eigenvalue barely above 1.0 and explained only

10.2 percent of the variance. Reliability analysis on the entire 10-item index produced a

Cronbach's alpha of .89. Deleting any of the 10 items would have decreased the reliability.

Therefore, a single-factor solution was suggested and the 10-item scale was retained as a

single measure of advertising believability. The average inter-item correlation for the 10

items was .45.

Candidate Evaluation Scale

Principal factor analysis of the 10-item candidate evaluation scale produced two

factors with Eigenvalues greater than 1.0. Six items clearly loaded on the first factor. The

remaining four items loaded on both factors but always more strongly on the first. The first

factor (Eigenvalue = 5.31) was clearly dominant, explaining 53.1 percent of the variance.

The second factor had an Eigenvalue barely above 1.0 and explained only 10.8 percent of

the variance. Reliability analysis produced a Cronbach's alpha of .90. Deleting any of the

10 items would have decreased the reliability. In addition, the average inter-item correlation for the scale was .48. Therefore, a single-factor solution was suggested and the 10-item scale was retained as a single measure of candidate evaluation.

Political Involvement Scale

The 11-item political involvement scale used as the independent variable in testing the research questions consisted of six measures designed to measure political activity and five items designed to measure political communication practices. Principal factor analysis for the five political communication measures produced only one factor with an Eigenvalue greater than 1. The one dominant factor (Eigenvalue = 2.87) explained 57.4 percent of the variance. Reliability analysis for the political communication items showed a Cronbach's alpha of .81 and an average inter-item correlation coefficient of .29. Principal factor analysis on the six items measuring political activity also revealed one dominant factor (Eigenvalue = 2.48), which explained 41.3 percent of the variance. Reliability on the activity scale was .69, with an inter-item correlation coefficient of .45. The reliability on the political activity measure would had dropped significantly if any of the items were deleted.

When the 11 items were tested as one scale, reliability improved to .84, with an average inter-item correlation of .32. Principal factor analysis on the combined scale produced two factors with Eigenvalues greater than 1. However, one factor was clearly dominant (Eigenvalue = 4.28) and explained 38.9 percent of the variance.[5] In addition, all of the 11 items loaded on this factor at .43 and higher. All but two loaded higher on the first

[5] The second factor was much smaller (Eigenvalue = 1.63) and explained only 14.8 percent of the variance.

factor than the second, further suggesting that the 11-items could be analyzed together as one measure.

To measure subjects' political involvement, scores on the 11 items were averaged for each subject. Following the procedure used in dividing the subjects on Need for Cognition scores, those with political involvement scores below 2.28 were classified as low in political involvement, while subjects scoring 2.28 or higher were classified as high in political involvement. The median split for political involvement produced two relatively equal-sized groups (n = 122, $\underline{M}$ = 1.91, $\underline{SD}$ = .30 for low political involvement; n = 120, $\underline{M}$ = 2.76, $\underline{SD}$ = .42 for high political involvement).[6]

Assumptions

Several assumptions made in designing the study were tested with the data collected. First, it was assumed that random assignment would lead to virtually equal treatment groups, a critical factor when using ANOVA. As Table 4-1 shows (see p. 107), all but one cell contained between 16 and 19 subjects. Second, the researcher assumed that the subject population would be relatively homogenous, allowing for an easier isolation of the treatment effects and the specific individual differences, namely need for cognition, being tested in this study. The demographic data presented above confirms this assumption. In addition, ANOVAs performed on the two dependent variables revealed no significant main effects for gender, age, or ideology.

---

[6] Two subjects did not fill out all of the items on the political involvement scale and therefore were deleted from the analysis with this measure.

It also was suspected that subjects would have little or no prior knowledge of the race or the candidates that would affect the two dependent measures, commercial and candidate evaluation. Data gathered during the experiment supported the assumption that few subjects would have prior knowledge of the campaign, the candidates, or the commercial used as a stimulus in the experiment. While 56 (22.9 percent) of the 244 subjects reported having heard of at least one of the candidates, 40 (71.4 percent) of those 56 said they had no pre-existing opinions of either candidate. Therefore, only 6.6 percent of the total subject pool held either favorable or unfavorable opinions about the candidate before participating in the experiment. Most of the 16 who said they had pre-existing opinions of the candidates reported relatively moderate views, stating that they either liked or disliked one of the candidates. Only five subjects total held extreme opinions of either candidate, either disliking very much or liking very much.[7]

It also was assumed during the design of the study that subjects would not be affected by the printed "(Dem.)" tag that appeared in the last five seconds of the Godbold commercial shown as a stimulus. To test this, evaluation of the commercial and the candidate were tested in a one-way ANOVA using political party as the independent variable. If subjects who reported being Democrats were aware of or affected by the Democratic label in the Godbold ad, they might have rated him more positively that those who identified themselves as Republicans. Interestingly, there was a significant main effect for party on the advertising believability measure (F (3, 219) = 2.63, p < .05.) However,

---

[7] Analyses of the data were conducted with and without these subjects. No difference in significance or direction of findings was found when testing the hypotheses and research questions without these subjects. Therefore, the findings reported in this chapter include these 16 subjects.

simple effects tests of the means revealed no significant difference between Democrats (M = 3.45) and Republicans (M = 3.36). The party identification that scored significantly different than the others was the "independent" category (M = 3.94). Independents evaluated the commercial as significantly more believable than Democrats (t (124) = 1.99, p. < .05), Republicans (t (112) = 2.18, p. < .05), and those marking "other" (M = 2.89) for political party (t (25) = 2.25, p. < .05). No significant differences were found between the "others" and the Republicans or Democrats. No significant party differences were found on the candidate evaluation scale.

If independents had been reacting to the party identification mark "(Dem.)" at the end of the commercial, they would be expected to rate the commercial more negatively, because they would have seen the candidate as tied to a political party. But because the Republicans and Democrats did not differ on the advertising believability measure, and because the independents rated the commercial more positively than the other groups, it can be assumed with some certainty that the "(Dem.)" tagline in the commercial went unnoticed by--or at the very least did not affect--the subjects in the study.

Manipulation Checks

Argument Quality

To develop adwatch arguments of varying levels of argument quality, a pilot test was conducted (see Chapter 3). The goal was to develop arguments that were viewed as significantly different from each other in perceived quality. The pilot test, however, measured differences within subjects, not between subjects as would be used in the experiment. Therefore, a manipulation check for argument quality was included at the end of the questionnaire. After subjects had been asked about the dependent variables and answered a few open-ended questions, they were instructed to think back to the information they were given in the newspaper article (the adwatch) about the Godbold commercial. Subjects then were asked to rate the arguments presented in the newspaper article. A four-item measure, identical to the one used in the pilot test of argument quality, was used. Subjects rated the arguments used in the adwatch on the following semantic differentials: Weak/Strong; Unconvincing/Convincing; Irrational/Rational; Not believable/Believable. Again, a seven-point scale, with 1 and 7 representing the extremes, was used to gauge attitudes.

A principal components factor analysis on the four-item argument quality measure produced one factor (Eigenvalue = 3.26), which explained 81.6 percent of the variance. Reliability analysis showed Cronbach's alpha of .92, which would have been reduced significantly if any item was dropped. An ANOVA testing argument quality by treatment group showed that the manipulation check for argument quality was successful between subjects in the various treatment groups. The six treatment groups were produced by a 2 (high or low argument quality) x 3 (pro-Godbold newspaper, anti-Godbold newspaper, no newspaper credibility cue) design. For the manipulation checks, ANOVAs were conducted with both argument quality and source credibility as independent variables to check for confounding manipulations. As expected, the manipulation check for argument quality showed a main effect for the groups getting either the high- or low-quality arguments. The 101 subjects who received the low-quality adwatch rated argument quality of the adwatch as significantly lower (M = 4.48) than the 97 subjects who received a high-quality adwatch ($M = 5.66$, F $(1, 192) = 47.67$, $p < .001$). This suggests that subjects were highly attuned to adwatch argument quality when evaluating the commercial and the sponsoring candidate.

However, in addition to the expected main effect for argument quality, a significant main effect also was found for source credibility in the argument-quality manipulation check (F $(2, 192) = 7.86$, $p < .001$.) Simple effects tests of the means in the three source credibility treatment groups showed that subjects in the anti-Godbold source credibility treatments evaluated argument quality as significantly lower ($M = 4.59$) than either those in the pro-Godbold condition ($M = 5.32$, t $(134) = 3.12$, $p < .003$) and those who were given no information about source credibility ($M = 5.30$, t $(130) = 3.01$, $p < .004$). No two-way interaction was found between argument quality and source credibility treatments, suggesting no confounding manipulations.

Source Credibility

Source credibility was manipulated by exposing different treatment groups to different newspaper objectivity cues: One group received a pro-Godbold cue, the second received an anti-Godbold cue, and the third received no objectivity information about the adwatch they read. It was thought that those receiving an adwatch from a "pro-Godbold" newspaper might evaluate the adwatch differently than those reading an adwatch in an "anti-Godbold" newspaper. Subjects would expect an adwatch in the anti-Godbold newspaper to attack the commercial. In contrast, subjects reading a pro-Godbold newspaper might see the adwatch source as more credible because the newspaper was attacking a candidate it consistently supported. Subjects were expected to concluded that the Godbold ad must be highly misleading to cause a supportive newspaper to turn on Godbold.

To test whether subjects attended to and remembered the newspaper objectivity section in evaluating the commercial and the candidate, subjects were asked near the end of the questionnaire to think about the newspaper article they read. Then subjects were asked: "Based on information you were given about the newspaper's objectivity, would you say the newspaper would be likely to support Godbold, be neutral, or support Delaney?" Subjects who chose support Godbold were coded as 1, neutral answers were coded as 2, and the support Delaney response was coded as 3. Subjects who received the pro-Godbold objectivity cue were expected to score lower on the measure than subjects who received the anti-Godbold objectivity cue.

As expected, all the three source credibility treatment conditions varied significantly in evaluating the objectivity of the newspaper. An ANOVA found a main effect for the source credibility treatment (F (2, 190) = 41.40, p < .001). Simple effects tests showed that the pro-Godbold condition (M = 1.84) rated the paper as more likely to support Godbold than either the anti-Godbold group (M = 2.50, t (132) = 9.23, p < .001) or the no information condition (M = 2.84, t (124) = 5.13, p < .001). While the pro-Godbold condition was expected to be closer to 1 on the measure, the presence of an adwatch in general, which attacks a candidate's claims, might make subjects think the paper is against the candidate regardless of the objectivity information presented. The ANOVA for the source credibility manipulation did not reveal any main effects for the argument quality conditions (high- or low-quality adwatch arguments). In addition, no two-way interactions between source credibility treatment groups and argument quality treatment groups emerged in the data analysis. The findings suggest that subjects did attend to and recall the newspaper objectivity cue.

After examining whether subjects attended to the newspaper objectivity statement in evaluating the commercial and the candidate, a test was conducted to check the assumption that varying newspaper objectivity was a manipulation of source credibility. In a separate pilot study, a smaller group of college students (n = 20) were asked to read one of the three newspaper objectivity statements, read the adwatch, then evaluate the credibility of the newspaper that printed the adwatch. Subjects in this between-subjects test of credibility were asked to rate the newspaper in which the adwatch appeared on three dimensions: Not Credible/Credible; Unbelievable/Believable; Untrustworthy/Trustworthy. Subjects were asked to score the semantic differentials on a seven-point response scale, with 1 and 7 representing the extremes. Because there was no interaction between argument quality and source credibility in source credibility manipulation check reported above, all subjects were given the high-quality adwatch to read in the independent check of source credibility.

It was suspected that subjects who received the pro-Godbold statement would rate the newspaper as more credible than subjects who received an anti-Godbold statement. No assumptions were made for the subjects who received no objectivity information about the newspaper before reading the adwatch. A one-way ANOVA conducted for the three newspaper objectivity conditions found no significant differences among the three groups. However, an examination of the group means found that subjects who received a pro-Godbold newspaper objectivity statement did see the adwatch source as more

credible (n = 8, $\underline{M}$ = 5.67) than those who received an anti-Godbold newspaper

objectivity cue (n = 7, $\underline{M}$ = 4.24, $\underline{t}$ = 2.06, $\underline{p}$ < .061). A test of the means between subjects

receiving no newspaper objectivity statement (n = 5, $\underline{M}$ = 4.13) and subjects receiving an

anti-Godbold objectivity statement ($\underline{M}$ = 4.24) showed no differences between the two

groups. Because the researcher had no expectations about subjects receiving no

newspaper objectivity statement, and because means in this group and the anti-Godbold

objectivity group were virtually identical, these two conditions were collapsed.

Comparing this larger group (n = 12, $\underline{M}$ = 4.19) with the pro-Godbold objectivity group

(n = 8, $\underline{M}$ = 5.67) showed significant differences in the direction expected ($\underline{t}$ = 2.28, p <

.04). Subjects receiving a pro-Godbold objectivity statement did rate the newspaper as

significantly more credible than subjects who read an adwatch but did not receive a pro-

Godbold cue. Therefore, the manipulation check for source credibility was successful.

Tests of Hypotheses

For illustration purposes only, an omnibus ANOVA was run for each dependent

variable by experimental condition and need for cognition. Mean scores of advertising

believability and candidate evaluation scores are reported in Table 4-1.

Main Effects Hypothesis

Two hypotheses were proposed to test the general question: Does exposure to an

adwatch make subjects more critical of the commercial being reviewed and the candidate

sponsoring the commercial targeted in the adwatch?

TABLE 4-1

Means for advertising believability and candidate evaluation measures
split by low/high need for cognition and experimental condition
(with cell size)

Experimental Condition	Advertising Believability Score		Candidate Evaluation Score	
	Low NFC	High NFC	Low NFC	High NFC
Control group (no adwatch)	3.64 (18)	4.00 (17)	3.71 (18)	4.02 (17)
High-Credibility/ High-quality	3.83 (16)	2.81 (19)	4.14 (16)	3.63 (19)
High-Credibility/ Low-quality	3.59 (18)	3.38 (17)	3.70 (18)	3.73 (17)
Low-Credibility (OC)/ High-quality	3.76 (17)	3.12 (18)	4.18 (17)	3.79 (18)
Low-Credibility (OC)/ Low-quality	3.58 (19)	3.55 (18)	3.98 (19)	4.10 (18)
Low-Credibility (NC)/ High-quality	3.51 (13)	3.03 (18)	3.77 (13)	3.68 (18)
Low-Credibility (NC)/ Low-quality	3.49 (15)	3.29 (18)	4.06 (15)	4.01 (18)
Totals:	3.63 (116)	3.30 (125)	3.93 (116)	3.85 (125)

KEY: OC = Subjects were provided with an objectivity cue about the newspaper;
NC = Subjects did not receive a cue about newspaper objectivity.

Note: Low scores on the advertising believability index and candidate evaluation measures indicate subjects viewed the commercial as not believable. Higher scores meant subjects found the commercial more believable. The scale was based on a seven-point response measure, with 1 being the lowest and 7 the highest.

H1: Subjects view a televised ad then read a newspaper adwatch will hold more negative attitudes about ad than subjects not exposed to an adwatch who view a televised ad and simply reread the text of the ad in print.

H2: Subjects view a televised ad then read a newspaper adwatch will hold more negative attitudes about the sponsoring candidate than subjects not exposed to an adwatch who view a televised ad and simply reread the text of the ad in print.

Stated simply, it was expected that subjects in the no-adwatch control condition would evaluate the commercial and the candidate more positively, and thus have higher average scores on the advertising believability scale and on the candidate evaluation measure than subjects in any of the six treatment groups, which were all exposed to an adwatch.

To test these two hypotheses, subjects receiving an adwatch (n = 206) were compared to subjects in the no-adwatch control group (n = 35) on each dependent measure. The ANOVA for the first dependent variable, advertising believability, showed that the treatment group ($\underline{M}$ = 3.40) rated the commercial as significantly less believable than the control group ($\underline{M}$ = 3.81, $\underline{F}$ (1, 239) = 5.12, $\underline{p}$. = .025). Therefore, Hypothesis 1 was supported. However, the data did not support Hypothesis 2. When the candidate evaluation measure was used as the dependent variable, no difference was found between the groups reading any type of adwatch ($\underline{M}$ = 3.90) and the no-adwatch control group ($\underline{M}$ = 3.86).

In the course of testing all hypotheses in this study, several significant main effects and interactions were discovered. For convenience, the results of all tests of hypotheses that produced showed differences at the $\underline{p}$ < .05 level of significance are presented in Table 4-2. Each of these findings also will be discussed in detail below.

Individual Differences

The study was designed to move beyond the basic question: Do adwatches work? The research examines under what conditions adwatches work or do not work. Three variables--subject's need for cognition, adwatch argument quality, and adwatch source credibility--were expected to interact to explain when adwatches can be effective in altering attitudes about candidates and their messages.

Adwatch argument quality

Two hypotheses were proposed to examine what effect manipulating adwatch argument quality might have on different types of subjects.

H3: Subjects who score high on a need for cognition measure who view an ad and then read a high-quality adwatch will hold more negative attitudes toward the ad than high-need-for-cognition subjects who view and ad and then read a low-quality adwatch. Subjects who score low in the need for cognition will be unaffected by argument quality in evaluating the commercial.

H4: Similarly, subjects who score high on a need for cognition measure who view an ad and then read a high-quality adwatch will hold more negative attitudes toward the sponsoring candidate than high-need-for-cognition subjects who view an ad and then read a low-quality adwatch. Again, subjects who score low in the need for cognition will be unaffected by argument quality in evaluating the sponsoring candidate.

Stated simply, it was expected that need-for-cognition would interact with adwatch argument quality, producing significant differences in high-need for-cognition subjects only. It was thought that high-need-for-cognition subjects exposed to a high-quality adwatch would have a lower average score on the advertising believably scale and the candidate evaluation measure than high-need-for-cognition subjects who saw a low-quality adwatch. The means for the low-need-for-cognition subjects were not expected to differ, regardless of adwatch quality. No main effects were expected for adwatch quality.

TABLE 4-2

Significant differences between means for the advertising believability measure

(Mean 1 > Mean 2)

	Mean 1	Mean 2	t	p ≤
Main effects				
H1: Main effect of adwatch[a]	No adwatch M = 3.81	Read adwatch M = 3.40	2.26	.026
Main effect of NFC[b]	Low NFC M = 3.63	High NFC M = 3.20	3.06	.003
NFC Interactions				
H3: NFC x AQ[b]	High NFC/Low AQ M = 3.41	High NFC/High AQ M = 2.98	2.08	.041
	High AQ/Low NFC M = 3.71	High AQ/High NFC M = 2.98	3.64	.001
H5: NFC x SC[b]	High SC/Low NFC M = 3.70	High SC/High NFC M = 3.08	2.50	.016
Research Questions: PI Interactions				
RQ (H3): PI x AQ[b]	High PI/Low AQ M = 3.59	High PI/Low AQ M = 3.03	2.77	.008

KEY: NFC = Need for Cognition; AQ = Adwatch Argument Quality; SC = Adwatch Source Credibility; PI = Political Involvement.

a = all subjects; b = all treatment groups, excluding the no-adwatch control group (M = 35).

To test these hypotheses, an ANOVA was run testing the dependent measures by using need for cognition, argument quality treatment groups, and source credibility treatment groups. As expected, no main effects emerged for source credibility or argument quality. No interactions--either two-way or three-way--were observed with source credibility. Therefore, all subjects receiving a high-quality adwatch (n = 101), regardless of source credibility treatment, were combined into one group for further analysis, as were all subjects receiving a low-quality adwatch (n = 105), also regardless of source credibility treatment.[8] Therefore, a 2 (high- or low-quality adwatch) x 2 (high- and low-need-for-cognition) design was tested. An ANOVA using advertising believability measure as the dependent variable found significant differences among the four means. A main effect for need for cognition was found ($\underline{F}$ (1, 202) = 9.57, $\underline{p}$. < .004). Low-need-for-cognition subjects rated the commercial as significantly more believable ($\underline{M}$ = 3.63) than high-need-for-cognition subjects ($\underline{M}$ = 3.19). A significant two-way interaction between cognition and argument quality ($\underline{F}$ (1, 202) = 4.32, $\underline{p}$. < .043) also was found.

To examine whether the means were significantly different in the ways predicted by Hypothesis 3, simple effects tests were performed. As predicted, the high-need-for-cognition subjects' evaluation of the commercial was dependent on the quality of adwatch they were exposed to. High-need-for-cognition subjects who read a low-quality

---

[8] The no-adwatch control group was omitted from this test and the rest of the tests of hypotheses, as the predicted differences were only between those groups receiving an adwatch. Removing the 35 subjects in the control group, plus three subjects who did not complete all items in the scales used as the dependent measures, left 206 subjects for the remaining tests of hypotheses.

adwatch ($\underline{M}$ = 3.41) rated the commercial as significantly more believable that high-need-for-cognition subjects who received a high-quality adwatch ($\underline{M}$ = 2.98, $\underline{t}$ (106) = 2.08, $\underline{p}$ < .02). Also as predicted, no differences were found in the means between the low-need-for-cognition scores, regardless of argument quality.[9] Therefore, Hypotheses 3 was supported by the data.

An interesting and unexpected finding emerged in testing the means for Hypotheses 3. While a main effect was reported for need for cognition, differences between low- and high-need-for-cognition subjects emerged only among subjects in the high-quality adwatch group. Of the 101 subjects who received a high-quality adwatch, the 55 high-need-for-cognition subjects rated the ad as significantly less believable ($\underline{M}$ = 2.98) than the 46 low-need-for-cognition subjects who received a high-quality adwatch ($\underline{M}$ = 3.71, $\underline{t}$ (99) = 3.64, p < .001). No differences emerged between low- and high-need-for-cognition subjects who received a low-quality adwatch ($\underline{M}$ = 3.56 versus $\underline{M}$ = 3.41).

While the data supported Hypothesis 3, no support was found for Hypothesis 4. An ANOVA using the candidate evaluation measure as the dependent variable and grouping subjects by adwatch quality and need for cognition found no main effects. In addition, no interaction between need for cognition and argument quality was found.[10] This analysis does support the prediction that attitudes of low-need-for-cognition subjects

---

[9] Low-need-for-cognition subjects receiving a low-quality adwatch had an average advertising believability score of 3.56, while low-need-for-cognition subjects receiving a high-quality adwatch had a mean score of 3.71.

[10] The means, however, were in the direction expected. High-need-for-cognition subjects who saw a low-quality adwatch rated the candidate as slightly higher ($\underline{M}$ = 3.95) than high-need-for-cognition subjects who saw a high-quality adwatch ($\underline{M}$ = 3.70).

would not be affected by argument quality. But the hypotheses relied on the differences

among high-need-for-cognition subjects that were not found.

Adwatch source credibility

Source credibility was manipulated in this study with a newspaper objectivity cue.

It was thought that a newspaper that routinely supported a candidate, then suddenly

questioned the accuracy of that candidate's ad claims, would be seen as credible. In

contrast, an adwatch by a newspaper that consistently attacks a candidate should be seen as

less credible. No predictions were made for subjects receiving no objectivity cue.

Two hypotheses were proposed to test this conceptualization of source credibility:

> H5: Low-need-for-cognition subjects who view an ad and then read an adwatch
> from a source that has consistently supported the candidate will hold more negative
> attitudes toward the ad than low-need-for-cognition subjects who view and ad and
> then read an adwatch from a source that has consistently attacked the candidate.
> High-need-for-cognition subjects will be unaffected by source credibility in
> evaluating the commercial.

> H6: Low-need-for-cognition subjects who view an ad and then read an adwatch
> from a source that has consistently supported the candidate will hold more negative
> attitudes toward the sponsoring candidate than low-need-for-cognition subjects who
> view and ad and then read an adwatch from a source that has consistently attacked
> the candidate. Again, high-need-for-cognition subjects will be unaffected by source
> credibility in evaluating the candidate.

As with the previous set of hypotheses, it was predicted that need-for-cognition and

adwatch source credibility would interact, but no interactions would emerge involving

argument quality. Low-need-for-cognition subjects who received a pro-Godbold newspaper

objectivity cue were expected to see the adwatch as more credible. Therefore, low-need-

for-cognition subjects reading an adwatch from a pro-Godbold newspaper would score

lower on the advertising believability scale and the candidate evaluation measure than low-need-for-cognition subjects who read an adwatch from an anti-Godbold newspaper. Because the results of the manipulation check for source credibility found no differences in perceived credibility between subjects receiving an anti-Godbold newspaper objectivity statement and no objectivity cue, these two groups were collapsed for further analysis of source credibility. Means for high-need-for-cognition subjects were not expected to be affected by the source credibility manipulation.

Again, an ANOVA was conducted using all three independent variables. As expected, argument quality did not interact with the source credibility treatment on any levels. Therefore, subjects were grouped regardless of argument quality into those who received a pro-Godbold objectivity statement (n = 70), who were expected see the newspaper as a credible source, and those who received an anti-Godbold objectivity statement or no objectivity statement (n= 136).[11]

An ANOVA testing advertising believability by source credibility showed no main effects for source credibility, as expected. However, a main effect did emerge for need for cognition. Subjects low in the need for cognition rated the ad as more believable (M = 3.63) than subjects high in the need for cognition (M = 3.19, F (1, 202) = 9.34, p < .004). Interestingly, simple effects tests showed that the difference reported for need for cognition was only significant in for subjects in the high source credibility groups. High-need-for-cognition subjects who received a pro-Godbold statement rated the commercial as significantly less believable (M = 3.08) than low-need for cognition subjects who read the same statement (M = 3.70, t (68) = 2.5, p < .016).

---

[11] Subjects in the no-adwatch control group were excluded from the analysis.

Hypothesis 5 was based on an expected two-way interaction between source credibility treatment group and need for cognition. However, no significant interaction between the need for cognition and source credibility measures was found. Simple effects tests of the means of the low-need-for-cognition groups found no significant difference between the high-source credibility treatment (M = 3.70) and low-source credibility treatment (M = 3.59). Hypotheses 5 also predicted that the source credibility cue would have no effect on subjects high in the need for cognition. No differences were found in the means on the advertising believability score for high-need-for-cognition subjects.

To test Hypothesis 6, the same ANOVA design was conducted using the candidate evaluation measure as the dependent variable. Although the means were in the direction expected, no main effects or interactions were found for candidate evaluation by need for cognition and source credibility manipulation. To further investigate the hypothesis, simple effects tests were conducted for among low-need-for-cognition subjects. Those in the high-source-credibility treatments did rate the candidate slightly lower (M = 3.91) than those in the low-source-credibility treatments (M = 4.01). However, these means were not significantly different, meaning Hypothesis 6 must be rejected. As with argument believability, no differences were found in high-need-for-cognition subjects, as expected.

Research Questions

To further test the application of the Elaboration Likelihood Model to adwatch effects research, the individual differences hypotheses were re-tested splitting subjects as high and low in political involvement, as opposed to need for cognition. Condra (1992) found that need for cognition was closely linked to political interest and activity. That relationship was tested in the current study in two ways. First, Condra's analytic technique was replicated to compare subjects' need for cognition scores and political involvement scores. An ANOVA was conducted testing subjects' average score on the 11-item political involvement scale and the 15-item Need for Cognition scale. As expected, subjects low in the need for cognition reported being significantly less involved in politics (n = 117, M = 2.18) than subjects high in the need for cognition (n = 125, M = 2.47, F (1, 240), = 5.36, p < .001).[12] The relationship between need for cognition and political involvement also was examined by a correlation analysis between subjects' scores on the two variables. The need for cognition score was highly correlated with the political involvement score (Pearson's correlation coefficient = .570). Finding a strong link between need for cognition and political involvement, all individual differences hypotheses (Hypothesis 3 through Hypothesis 6) were re-tested with political involvement as the moderating variable. The results were nearly identical to those found when testing the hypotheses using need for cognition as the moderator.

To re-test Hypotheses 3, advertising believability was tested by adwatch argument quality and political involvement. As expected, no main effects emerged for the argument quality manipulation or for political involvement. Also as expected, a significant two-way interaction emerged between argument quality and political involvement (F (1, 201) = 7.28, p < .009). Simple effects tests showed no differences in

---

[12] Two subjects did not complete all items in the political involvement scale and were deleted from further analysis.

subjects low in political involvement, as predicted. However, subjects scoring high in political involvement who received a low-quality adwatch rated the commercial as significantly more believable ($\underline{M}$ = 3.59) than highly politically involved subjects who read a low-quality adwatch ($\underline{M}$ = 3.03, t (99) = 2.77, p < .008). Therefore, Hypothesis 3 tested with political involvement as the moderating variable was supported.

Hypothesis 4, which tested the same ANOVA design using the candidate evaluation measure as the dependent variable, was not supported when subjects were divided by need for cognition. However, splitting subjects by political involvement did so some differences. No main effect was found for political involvement on the candidate evaluation measure, as expected. However, a two-way interaction approaching significance was observed between the political involvement of the subjects and the quality of adwatch argument that they were exposed to (F (1,201) = 2.89, p < .073). To further examine the relationship between the two variables, means were compared with simple effects tests. No differences were found within either the low political involvement subjects or within the high political involvement subjects, regardless of adwatch quality. However, a significant difference was observed within the high-adwatch-quality treatment condition. Low-political-involvement subjects who read a high-quality adwatch rated the candidate more favorably ($\underline{M}$ = 4.05) than high-political-involvement subjects receiving the same quality adwatch ($\underline{M}$ = 3.68), t (99) = 1.95, p < .054). But because this was not the interaction suggested by the Hypothesis 4, the hypothesis was not supported.

Examining the source credibility hypotheses (5 and 6) splitting subjects by political involvement instead of need for cognition produced no significant differences-- for main effects, two-way interactions, and simple effects tests--among treatment groups on the two dependent measures. Again, while no differences were found among subjects high in political involvement as predicted, no differences emerged when testing the low-political-involvement subjects, who were predicted to differ on the measures depending on source credibility treatment. Therefore, the research questions were not supported.

A final research question examined reported voting intentions of subjects. Ansolabehere and Iyengar (1995) found that exposure to an adwatch produced a "boomerang" effect, causing subjects who viewed an adwatch to be more likely to vote for the candidate whose ad was being critiqued in the adwatch. In the current study, comparing subjects who received an adwatch to those who did not receive an adwatch did reveal significant differences in voting intention. But contrary to Ansolabehere and Iyengar's findings, subjects who read an adwatch after viewing the commercial were significantly less likely to vote for Godbold ($\underline{M}$ = 2.63) than subjects who did not read an adwatch ($\underline{M}$ = 3.47, $\underline{F}$ (1, 101) = 10.57, $\underline{p}$ < .003).[13]

A summation of the findings for the hypotheses and research questions is presented in the next chapter, along with a discussion of the results, noted limitations of the study, practical applications of the findings, and suggestions for future research.

---

[13] These results are based only on the subjects who received a five-point voting intention scale (n = 103), where 1 indicated that the subject would definitely vote for Delaney and 5 indicated the subject would definitely vote for Godbold.

CHAPTER V
DISCUSSION

This dissertation investigated the effects of adwatch exposure on attitudes toward political advertisements and their sponsoring candidates. In addition to examining the overall effect of exposure to an adwatch, the research was designed to examine the conditions under which adwatches might be more effective in shaping the attitudes of certain groups of individuals.

Three groups of related research hypotheses, six in all, were presented in detail in Chapter II to predict the effects of three independent variables on two dependent variables. The independent variables under investigation were subjects' need for cognition, adwatch argument quality, and adwatch source credibility. The dependent measures tested were advertising believability and candidate evaluation.

The key findings that emerged from tests of these hypotheses are summarized below. The summary is followed by post-hoc analyses designed to shed light on the findings. Limitations and problems with the research are presented, followed by implications of the research. The dissertation concludes with suggestions for future research.

Summary of Results

Tests of Hypotheses

The first group of hypotheses suggested that mere exposure to an adwatch, regardless of individual differences in subjects or characteristics of the adwatch, would cause subjects to evaluate the commercial and its sponsoring candidate more critically than subjects who were not exposed to an adwatch. Subjects reading an adwatch did evaluate the commercial as less believable than those who did not read an adwatch. However, no differences in candidate evaluation emerged.

The second group of hypotheses investigated the effects of the interaction of need for cognition and argument quality on the commercial and candidate evaluation measures. As predicted, subjects high in the need for cognition looked to adwatch argument quality in evaluating the commercial. High-need-for-cognition subjects who read a high-quality adwatch rated the commercial as significantly less believable than high-need-for-cognition subjects who read a low-quality adwatch. Also as predicted, adwatch argument quality had no effect on how subjects low in the need for cognition evaluated advertising believability. As with the first set of hypotheses, no significant differences in candidate evaluation were found.

The third group of hypotheses investigated the effects of the interaction of need for cognition and source credibility on the commercial and candidate evaluation measures. Source credibility did not affect how subjects low in the need for cognition evaluated the commercial, in contrast to what the hypotheses predicted. As predicted, however, source credibility had no effect on how high-need-for-cognition subjects evaluated the commercial. No significant differences in candidate evaluation emerged.

Research Questions

Research questions examined the same questions asked by the hypotheses using different variables. The first set of hypotheses, which tested whether exposure to an adwatch affected the way subjects evaluated the commercial and candidate, was re-tested with a vote intention measure as the dependent variable. Consistent with the findings in Hypothesis 1, this analysis found that subjects exposed to an adwatch said they would be less likely to vote for the commercial's sponsoring candidate than subjects who did not read an adwatch.

The second set of hypotheses was re-tested splitting subjects by political involvement instead of need for cognition as an independent variable. Consistent with the findings of the hypotheses tests and other research linking political involvement and need for cognition, subjects high in political involvement looked to adwatch argument quality in evaluating the commercial. High-political-involvement subjects who read a high-quality adwatch rated the commercial as significantly less believable than high-political-involvement subjects who read a low-quality adwatch. Also as predicted, adwatch argument quality had no effect on how subjects low in political involvement viewed the commercial's believability. No significant differences in candidate evaluation were found.

Finally, the third set of hypotheses was re-tested with subjects again split into high- and low-political-involvement groups. As suspected, source credibility had no effect on how highly politically involved subjects evaluated the commercial. However, source credibility also did not affect how subjects low in political involvement evaluated the commercial. Again, no significant differences in candidate evaluation were measured.

In sum, the relationships predicted by previous adwatch studies and the Elaboration Likelihood Model of persuasion were supported in part. Data analysis showed that subjects exposed to an adwatch rated the commercial as less believable and reported a lower likelihood of voting for the ad's sponsoring candidate than subjects not exposed to an adwatch. In addition, adwatch argument quality affected the way subjects high in the need for cognition and those high in political involvement evaluated the commercial. However, the data analysis showed no support for the predictions that subjects low in the need for cognition and low in political involvement would look to source credibility in evaluating the ad. Throughout the analysis, evaluation of the candidate was not affected in any way by the manipulations.

Post-Hoc Analysis

Unexpected Findings

Tests of the hypotheses and the research questions also produced a finding not predicted at the start of this research. It was predicted that exposure to any adwatch would cause subjects to rate a political commercial as less believable than subjects not exposed to an adwatch. Interestingly, while a main effect for adwatch exposure was found as expected, it was not uniform in all subjects. Exposure to an adwatch appears only to have affected the way subjects high in the need for cognition viewed the commercial, as suggested by some of the unexpected findings discussed in Chapter IV.

To further investigate these findings, a post-hoc analysis of the interaction between adwatch exposure and need for cognition was conducted. As in testing the first set of hypotheses, subjects exposed to any adwatch were combined into one group and compared to subjects in the no-adwatch control group. Comparing the two groups on the advertising believability measure produced a significant interaction between need for cognition and adwatch exposure (F (1, 237) = .027, p < .028). Simple effects tests showed that high-need-for-cognition subjects who read an adwatch rated the commercial as significantly less believable (M = 3.19) than high-need-for cognition subjects who did not read an adwatch (M = 4.00, t (123) = 2.98, p < .004). No significant differences were reported among low-need-for-cognition subjects, regardless of whether they were exposed to an adwatch or not. In short, exposure to an adwatch affected attitudes only in high-need-for-cognition subjects, while adwatch exposure appears to have had no effect on low-need-for-cognition subjects.

Candidate Evaluation Measure

Throughout the research design, no significant results emerged in examining the candidate evaluation measure. Both political advertising and adwatch research studies have shown that the evaluation of the candidate sponsoring an attack ad can be affected by exposure to the ad, a counter ad, or an adwatch critique of the ad. This study, in contrast, found no effect of adwatch exposure on subjects' attitude toward the sponsoring candidate. In addition, no interactions between need for cognition, adwatch argument quality, and adwatch source credibility affected views toward the candidate.

Several explanations could be offered for the lack of differences found in candidate evaluation throughout the design. First, with the anti-politician mind-set that was prevalent at the time this study was conducted, a "basement" effect of candidate evaluation might have limited any effects exposure to an adwatch might have produced. In other words, if all subjects held an overwhelmingly negative view of the sponsoring candidate or of politicians in general, the candidate evaluation score would be so low that there would be virtually no room for change caused by a stimulus. However, a check of the data collected in this study suggests this was not the case. First, only 12 of the 244 subjects in the study reported that they had heard of Jake Godbold and disliked him. Only one subject reported disliking Godbold "very much."[1] In addition, mean candidate evaluation scores for the seven experimental groups in this study ranged from 3.71 to 4.04, all very close to the neutral mid-point of 4 on the candidate evaluation scale.

A more plausible explanation for why no differences in candidate evaluation were measured comes from looking at the content of the political commercial. As was noted in Chapter III, the sponsoring candidate, Jake Godbold, does not appear at all in the ad except for a small head shot at the bottom of the screen during the last four seconds of the ad. In contrast, Godbold's opponent, John Delaney, appears throughout the ad. In addition, except for one statement about Godbold cutting the number of city workers, all

---

[1] As reported in Chapter VI, tests of the hypotheses were conducted with and without the subjects who reported holding prior attitudes toward the candidates. Removing these subjects from the analysis produced no changes in significance or direction of the findings.

of the claims made in the ad pertain to John Delaney's record. Even though subjects were given a biographical sketch on Jake Godbold, they might not have received enough information about him from the commercial or the adwatch to form an opinion of him one way or the other. The clustering of mean candidate evaluation scores around the mid-point on the scale might suggest this to be the case.

Finally, it is possible that subjects did see Godbold as personally responsible for the claims made in the ad. It was assumed in designing this study--and apparently supported by the data--that subjects would not notice the tagline at the end of the commercial that identified it as a paid political ad by Jake Godbold. Several studies in recent years have documented a "backlash" or "boomerang" effect of attack advertising, in which negative political advertising exerts a negative influence on viewers' evaluations of sponsor (Garramone, 1984; Merritt, 1984). However, other research has shown that the boomerang effect is not universal (Johnson-Cartee & Copeland, 1991; Weigold, 1992). Recent studies have suggested that negative appeals can be used at little or no cost to the sponsoring candidate, especially when the audience does view the candidate as personally responsible for the attacks made in the ad (Weigold, 1991). Therefore, while this study found no significant effects of the manipulations of the independent variables on sponsoring candidate evaluation, other studies using a commercial in which the sponsoring candidate appears might produce different results.

Source Credibility Manipulation

Throughout this study, the manipulation of source credibility failed to produce any differences in subjects' attitudes. These lack of findings are problematic given that the Elaboration Likelihood Model is based on two assumptions: 1) Subjects highly involved in an issue or high in the need for cognition will look to argument quality in evaluating the persuasiveness of a message--a finding replicated in this study; and 2) subjects not involved in an issue or low in the need for cognition will look to peripheral cues such as source credibility in evaluating an advocacy--a finding not replicated by this research. Several explanations might be offered as to why subjects low in the need for cognition did not respond to the source credibility manipulation as predicted.

First, it could be argued that the manipulation of source credibility was too subtle. However, an independent check of the manipulation with a different subject pool did find that subjects receiving an adwatch from a "pro-Godbold" newspaper rated the newspaper as significantly more credible than other subjects. Another explanation for the lack of significance produced by the source credibility manipulation could be that subjects low in the need for cognition were not closely attuned to the manipulation check. As discussed in Chapter IV, all subjects who received a "pro-Godbold" source credibility cue rated the newspaper on average ($M = 1.84$) as closer to the "neutral" point of two on the three-point scale in the source credibility manipulation check than the "support Godbold" statement (which was scored as one). To test whether low-need-for-cognition subjects were less attuned to the manipulation, subjects who received a source credibility cue again were divided by need for cognition. If low-need-for-cognition subjects did not pay attention to the newspaper objectivity statement, they would have been less likely to correctly identify the newspaper as either "pro-Godbold" or "anti-Godbold" than their high-need-for-cognition counterpoints. An ANOVA of the source credibility measure tested by need for cognition and newspaper objectivity treatment found that this was not

the case. While high-need-for-cognition subjects were slightly better at identifying the

direction of the newspaper's support (either "pro-Godbold" or "anti-Godbold") than low-

need-for-cognition subjects, the means were not significantly different.

A third explanation why the source credibility manipulation did not produce the

predicted results could be that low-need-for-cognition subjects did not pay attention to

the entire newspaper stimulus presented after the ad, and instead rated the commercial

only on their impressions of the ad. Some support for this explanation comes in

examining the advertising believability measure by cognition and exposure to an

adwatch.[2] Subjects high in the need for cognition who saw an adwatch of any type rated

the commercial significantly lower than high-need-for-cognition subjects in the no-

adwatch control (t (123) = 2.98, p < .004). Low-need-for-cognition subjects, in contrast,

rated the believability of the ad as virtually the same whether they saw an adwatch of any

type (M = 3.63) or were in the no-adwatch control group (M = 3.64). This finding

suggests that exposure to an adwatch appears to have made no difference for low-need-

for-cognition subjects in evaluating the commercial.

To further examine whether low-need-for-cognition subjects relied on the

objectivity cue or on the adwatch in general in evaluating the commercial, a question was

included after the voting intention measure asking subjects which information most

helped them decide how to vote in the election. Subjects could select one of four options:

1) biographical information provided about the candidates; 2) information contained in

---

[2] See discussion in the Unexpected Results section above.

Godbold's television commercial; 3) information contained in the newspaper story about the ad (the adwatch); and 4) information provided about the newspaper's objectivity. A chi-square analysis on this response by cognition revealed significant differences in the types of information high- and low-need-for-cognition subjects used to form opinions about the race ($\chi^2 = 8.11$, $p < .044$).

The analysis showed that subjects low in the need for cognition were most likely than high-need-for-cognition subjects to rely on information presented in the television commercial itself and on information about the newspaper's objectivity.[3] In contrast, high-need-for-cognition subjects were more likely than low-need-for-cognition subjects to rely on biographical information about the candidates and on information in the adwatch. Of subjects low in the need for cognition, 39 percent said they relied on the candidate biographies, 21 percent relied on the ad, 28 percent relied on the adwatch, and 12 percent relied on the newspaper objectivity statement. Of subjects high in the need for cognition, 52 percent said they relied on the candidate biographies, 13 percent relied on the ad, 31 percent relied on the adwatch, and 4 percent relied on the newspaper objectivity statement.

A final explanation that may be offered for the lack of significant findings for the source credibility manipulation is perhaps the most plausible, given the theoretical framework of the study. The adwatch examined in this study, like most adwatches, conveys a negative message about the ad it is evaluating in that it attacks the accuracy of

---

[3] Of the 221 subjects who were included in this analysis, only 18 total said they made their voting choice based on the newspaper's objectivity. Of those 18, 13 were low-need-for-cognition subjects, while five were high-need-for-cognition subjects.

the claims made in the ad. The conclusion in both the low-quality and high-quality adwatches is that the Jake Godbold commercial distorts the facts. Previous research has found that source credibility is a less important determinant of persuasion for messages that are negative rather than positive. For example, Kanouse (1984) found that variance in source credibility is more significant in moderating positive appeals than negative appeals and that negative messages may be more credible than positive one. With positive messages, audience acceptance of the advocacy is a direct function of source credibility and believability. In contrast, source credibility appears unrelated to message acceptance for negative messages. Therefore, in negative communication situations, untrustworthy or inexpert sources can be just as potent as highly credible sources (Weigold, 1993).

This final suggestion for the lack of source credibility findings in the study is consistent with the ELM and has significant implications for adwatches. As content analyses have shown, most adwatches critiquing a specific ad are overwhelmingly negative because they conclude that the ad is misleading or false. This mainly is a function of the fact that adwatches tend to critique attack and issue-oriented ads more than positive and image-building ads. In this respect, the findings of this study might indicate that source credibility of the news organization producing an adwatch might not have any effect on the ability of the adwatch to affect voters' attitudes.

Problems and Limitations

The Subjects

An experimental design was selected for this study because of its power to explore and explain relationships between variables. The design was fully crossed with random assignment to treatment conditions to ward off many of the threats to internal validity (Cook & Campbell, 1979). External validity, defined as the ability to generalize experimental findings beyond conditions in a particular study, is more problematic in this type of research. The subjects used in this study, college students, are not representative of all U.S. voters who might be exposed to adwatches. In fact, they might not even be representative of all college students, given that the subjects came from an introductory advertising class. Subjects also were offered extra credit on an exam to participate in the study. In theory, the extra-credit award might have attracted only students struggling in the class.[4] If only students struggling in the class participated in the study, the subjects might not even represent a strong cross section of the students in the introductory advertising class. Therefore, caution should be urged in generalizing the findings of this study to other populations. The strong findings, however, suggest relationships that should be examined with other subject populations.

The Commercial

Another threat to external validity comes from the stimulus used in this experiment. While care was taken to assign subjects to treatment groups randomly, the commercial was not randomly selected. While the researcher viewed the commercial as

---

[4] Most instructors, however, argue this is not the case. Students at all levels of class performance tend to participate in extra-credit opportunities.

typical of advertising used in local election campaigns, the ad may not be representative of the type of political advertising that adwatches routinely critique. The fact that The Florida Times-Union did run an adwatch on the commercial used in the ad suggests that the research was replicating a "real-world" situation. In addition, the content analyses discussed in Chapter II suggested that most adwatches critique negative political commercials--or attack ads--the type of commercial used in this study.

This study also tested only one commercial and only one adwatch. In a typical election campaign, voters see a wide array of attacks and counter-attacks in political advertising. Exposing subjects to several commercials and several adwatches during an experiment might produce different results.

The Media

This study looked only at a televised commercial and only at a print adwatch. Most previous adwatch studies have examined televised commercials critiqued by televised adwatches. Only one other study to date (O'Sullivan & Geiger, 1995) has examined newspaper adwatches. It is highly likely that the results obtained in this study could be unique to newspaper critiques of televised ads. The results may not hold true for televised adwatches or even for newspaper adwatches of non-televised candidate advertising.

The Setting

Experiments have been criticized because of the artificiality of their setting, which also can threaten the ability of the study to describe the "real world." In this experiment, subjects watched one television ad in a large university classroom and then were told to read a newspaper article about the commercial. Obviously, this does not replicate how most voters are exposed to political advertising and adwatches. In the "real world," voters see the same political advertisement several times over several days. One ad may be run several times within a limited block of programming on one evening. Adwatches of specific commercials, in contrast, are published or broadcast once time. This study gave exposure to adwatches and political television commercials equal footing.

In addition, voters typically do not sit down and read an adwatch right after viewing an ad. If they read an adwatch about a commercial, it may be only after several exposures to the commercial. Some voters actually come into contact with an adwatch critique of the ad before they've seen the actual ad being reviewed by the news organization. And most likely, many voters never are exposed to the adwatch at all.

Implications

Despite the limitations of the study, the findings are helpful in understanding how exposure to adwatches can affect attitudes toward the political commercials they are reviewing. First and foremost, the results suggest that adwatches can be viewed as persuasive messages. The fact that exposure to an adwatch affected subjects' attitudes, even in a laboratory setting, suggests that adwatches can influence attitudes toward candidate messages contained in a commercial. After all, if no effect of adwatch exposure had been documented in a highly controlled setting, the power of adwatches to shape attitudes in a "real-world" setting--where subjects might not see or read an adwatch until several days after exposure to the ad--would be highly questionable. The results of the experiment suggest that adwatches can have some influence on voter attitudes toward

a commercial, at least in a laboratory setting.

The experimental findings also suggest that adwatches have the potential to work

as persuasive messages in some circumstances. While exposure to an adwatch appears to

make subjects more critical of that ad, a closer look at the results indicates that this effect

is not uniform among all subjects. In this study, exposure to an adwatch only affected

subjects high in the need for cognition. Subjects low in the need for cognition held the

same attitudes toward the commercial whether they were exposed to an adwatch or not.

This result is significant for two reasons. First, journalists say adwatches are

designed to help all voters make sense of the political process. But some journalists

argue that adwatches could have the greatest potential to help voters who are uninterested

in politics or who are unwilling to make the effort to examine ad claims in a given

election (for example, see Wolinsky et al., 1991). This study indicates that adwatches,

even in a controlled laboratory setting where subjects are exposed to messages with little

distraction, may have no effect on the uninterested or unmotivated voter, as demonstrated

by the fact that low-need-for-cognition subjects held exactly the same attitudes toward the

ad whether they read an adwatch or not.

Second, while the results indicate that adwatches have better success at

influencing voters who have the motivation and ability to process information about the

election, these may be the voters who are uninterested in seeking out adwatch information

in making voting choices. These type of voters, because of their interest in elaborating on

issues in a political campaign, might feel confident in their ability to form evaluations about a commercial without the help of the news media. Therefore, voters high in the need for cognition, or similarly highly interested in a race, might be less likely than voters low in the need for cognition, or those uninterested in a race, to seek out or pay attention to adwatches.

To test whether this might be the case, a measure was included in the experiment. The last item on the questionnaire asked subjects: "How likely would you be to read this type of article in the newspaper during an election campaign?" Subjects could choose from: 1) Very likely, 2) Somewhat likely, 3) Not at all likely. As suspected, subjects high in the need for cognition said they would be less likely ($M = 1.59$) to read an adwatch than subjects low in the need for cognition ($M = 1.84$, $F(1,96) = 3.69$, $p < .058$).[5] Therefore, it could be suggested that the type of voters most likely to be affected by adwatches might be least likely to seek them out and attend to them in "real-world" settings.

The study further suggests that adwatch influence is not guaranteed even with high-need-for-cognition subjects who actually attend to an adwatch. The results for the manipulation of argument quality show that high-need-for-cognition subjects were influenced only by an adwatch if the argument quality presented in the adwatch was high. This finding suggests that only high-quality adwatches have the potential to influence attitudes about a commercial or candidates. The implications for newspapers publishing

---

[5] While this difference is only approaching significance, a more sensitive measure might have produced significant differences. This question only was asked of the 123 subjects who participated in the experiment during March.

adwatches are clear: For adwatches to have any impact on any part of the audience, they must be seen as being of high quality by the readers.

It is interesting to note at this point that the actual adwatch arguments published in The Florida Times-Union as a critique of the commercial used in this study were examined in the pilot test of argument quality (see Appendix E for the actual adwatch that reviewed the ad). Each of the arguments that actually appeared in the newspaper scored nearer to the low-quality arguments used in this study than the high-quality arguments. If the Times-Union adwatch is typical of adwatches that appear in local newspapers, it could be suggested that typical newspaper adwatches might not affect any voter. Low-need-for-cognition subjects were not affected by exposure to adwatches in general, while high-need-for-cognition subjects were influenced only by a high-argument-quality adwatch. In other words, a low-quality adwatch might not be worth the paper it's printed on.

These findings have much to offer professional journalists as they gear up to cover another presidential campaign in 1996. The results presented above might paint a grim picture: Adwatches can only affect the attitudes of a limited number of voters under limited circumstances. But this finding only tells part of the picture. First, adwatches may have impacts in the political arena far beyond the scope of this study, which only examined the influence adwatches on audience attitudes toward the specific advertisement critiqued. Exposure to adwatches might make voters view the importance of political advertising in general differently, change attitudes toward the role of the media, examine the electoral process in a new light, or reconsider their own role in a democratic society. Adwatches also could have vast influence beyond the voters. In addition to assisting the voters, adwatches are designed to serve as checks on the candidates and their campaign staffs. This function goes to the heart of journalists' role as watchdogs. As one television newsman said of adwatches: "Our coverage is keeping the bastards honest" (Times Mirror, 1993, p. 3).[6] Obviously, the impact of the "truth squads" on the candidates and the campaigns is outside the scope of this study. Further research could examine whether adwatch effects were more powerful with the political elites than the average voter.

Viewed in a more positive light, the findings suggest that while adwatches might not be effective in helping all voters more critically evaluate an ad, the features might be of some use to some voters. For this influence to occur, the arguments rebutting an ad's claims must be seen as being of high quality. Journalists struggling with deadlines and space constraints might argue that producing high-quality adwatches is easier said than done. While researchers have the luxury of pre-testing arguments to come up with high quality arguments, journalists typically have only a few hours--or at the most a day--to produce an adwatch.

One suggestion for improving the chances that adwatches produced are of high quality is to ensure that a qualified staff writer or editor be placed in charge of adwatches. Adwatches, which do not appear on the front page and often do not carry a byline, may not be seen as the most glamorous assignment at newspapers. The Florida Times-Union,

---

[6] See Chapter I for the full quote.

for example, routinely had a reporting intern compile the information for its adwatches during the Godbold-Delaney race.

Adwatch quality also might better be ensured by turning the whole function over to outside experts. One Texas television station during the 1990 races hired a political science professor at a nearby university to critique political commercials (Wolinsky et al., 1991). The standard adwatch feature also could be turned over to the competing political parties, with each party receiving a limited amount of time or space to critique the other's ads. While this would take the adwatches out of the hands of "objective" journalists, this study's findings suggest that the credibility of the source producing the adwatch might have little effect--if any--on the ability of adwatches to influence attitudes about the candidates and the claims they make televised ads. If the goal of journalists is to help produce more informed voters, the source of the adwatch information should be secondary to the end result the feature is designed to accomplish.

Providing space for an outside "expert" or for political parties to critique campaign ads could serve the same function as current adwatches and remove journalists from their new position as "referee down on the field," returning them to the booth for color commentary (Rosenstiel, 1993, p. 273). Ironically, inviting partisan commentators to critique ads would move journalists back to their ideal of "objective" coverage of a race in that they would be relieved of having to judge claims as being true or false. An outside voice critiquing ads would return political advertising coverage to the more traditional function of journalism--to show as many perspectives on an issue or event as possible, allowing the audience to construct their own "reality" or "truth" from the information provided.

To compete in a profit-driven industry, news organizations often feel pressure to start new features, play new roles, and offer new services simply to keep up with the competition. As a result, those running the news organizations often do not have the luxury to reflect on the changes until after they have become well established, at which point they are very difficult to change. This may have been the case with adwatches. The features were introduced in 1990 by a limited number of news outlets, which received accolades from the industry and outside observers. Many other outlets took notice and followed suit throughout the first half of the decade. Now, four years after adwatches became a well-established feature in media coverage of U.S. elections, journalists should step back and assess the feature. The results of this research suggest two lines of inquiry for journalists producing adwatches. First, are adwatches worth the time, resources, and space that have been devoted to them in the past? This study indicates that adwatches affect only a limited number of voters in limited circumstances. Second, and perhaps more important, is producing adwatches a "proper" role for the press to play in elections? This research demonstrated that adwatches could have a function very similar to counter-attack advertising in helping voters reassess claims made in a political attack ad. This finding might indicate that campaign journalism has moved away from its ideal of "objective" coverage of a race.

Future Research

This study should be seen as only one small step of the many needed to understand the role that adwatches play in shaping attitudes toward candidates and their commercials. In analyzing the data and reviewing the results, several questions emerged that further research on adwatch effects might answer.

First, the influence of adwatch source credibility remains a question mark. More study is needed to examine whether the source credibility manipulation in this study was simply not successful or whether source credibility is not a factor in evaluating adwatch effects in general, especially when the messages carried by the adwatches are negative. A study examining source credibility that manipulated the message in the adwatch as either positive or negative might help lay this question to rest. Source credibility also might be re-examined through a manipulation in which the adwatch is said to come from either an "objective" news organization or from an opposing political camp.

The candidate evaluation measure also should be re-evaluated to determine whether the findings in this study can be generalized. To re-test candidate evaluation, a study could be designed in which subjects are shown an ad with the sponsoring candidate featured prominently or one in which the sponsoring candidate is not pictured. This type of research could shed light on whether subjects hold candidates personally responsible for ad claims targeted by adwatches. Further study using the candidate evaluation measure as a dependent variable might indicate whether adwatches affect attitudes about candidates sponsoring the commercial or only about the commercial that adwatches directly critique.

The theoretical framework used in this study also might prove useful in investigating whether effects of adwatch exposure are enduring. This study examined the effect of an adwatch immediately after subjects viewed an ad and read an adwatch. This study did not examine whether the effects of adwatch exposure are long-lasting or fleeting. Past studies using the Elaboration Likelihood Model have suggested that attitude change induced via the central route tends to be more enduring. Therefore, it could be assumed that high-need-for-cognition subjects who formed attitudes on the basis of argument quality might be more likely to hold the enduring attitudes toward the commercial (and possibly toward the candidate). Research re-testing subjects several times over a longer period after exposure to adwatches would be especially useful in answering examining the long-term effects of adwatches.

An even more interesting question, in light of the type of communication being studied, is whether central-route processing of adwatch information is more predictive of future behavior, as the ELM suggests. In political campaigns, favorable or unfavorable attitudes about a candidate are of no consequence if they do not translate into votes. A study examining adwatch exposure in an on-going political contest might be the best route in which to pursue this research question. Experimental manipulations, however, might be less successful in an on-going campaign in which subjects are constantly bombarded with other political communications outside of a laboratory setting.

While this study examined need for cognition, many ELM studies have used involvement as the variable moderating the route in which information will be processed.

An on-going campaign might provide the perfect venue for future studies examining the role of involvement as a moderator in elaboration on adwatch argument quality.

The current research begins to shed light not just on whether adwatches affect attitudes toward political commercials but also the factors that influence whether attitude change occurs. The study produced some findings not found in previous adwatch research. First, exposure to an adwatch appears to affect attitudes only of high-need-for-cognition voters, while low-need-for-cognition voters seem to be unaffected by a news organization's critical evaluation of an ad. In addition, the effect of adwatches on high-need-for-cognition subjects is not absolute. Only high-quality adwatches seem to work as journalists say they are intended--that is to make voters more critical of false or misleading ad claims. This study's application of a persuasion theory, the ELM, to adwatch effects research clears a new path for study that shows great promise in helping journalists, voters, and researchers understand the influence of this emerging form of political communication.

APPENDIX A
INFORMED CONSENT FORM

**PLEASE DO NOT TURN THIS PAGE
UNTIL YOU HAVE READ THESE INSTRUCTIONS**

INFORMED CONSENT

I am a graduate student at the University of Florida. As part of my dissertation research, I am gathering data from individuals on political advertising.

You are invited to participate in a study on political advertising. Your participation is voluntary and is important in helping me evaluate the ads. You do **not** have to answer any questions you do not wish to answer. Your instructor has agreed to give you two points extra credit toward one of your class exams for your participation. However, you will **not** receive financial compensation for your participation. This experiment should take no more than 25 minutes.

At places in the questionnaire, you will be asked to write the last six digits of your social security number along with your first and middle initials. The numbers will be torn off the questionnaire once I have finished, and no one will be able to link your answers to you. Your confidentiality is assured.

If at any time while you are involved in this study you wish to stop, you may do so. You are under no obligation to continue. If you would like any additional information, please contact: Dr. Michael Weigold, who is supervising this study, 2018 Weimer, phone 392-8199.

Please complete this portion:

I have read and have received a copy of this description. I agree to participate in the study as outlined above.

_____

participant's signature

_____

participant's printed name

_____

date

THANK YOU FOR YOUR HELP. PLEASE REMOVE THIS SHEET FROM THE QUESTIONNAIRE AND GIVE BOTH TO ONE OF THE ASSISTANTS WHEN YOU ARE FINISHED.

Approved by the University of Florida Institutional Review Board for use through February 21, 1997

John Delaney

Age: 38.

Family: Married with two daughters and one son.

Education: J.D. from Stetson University, B.A. in history from the University of North Florida.

Occupation: Attorney.

Military Experience: None.

Government Experience: General counsel, 1993-1994; chief of staff, Mayor's Office, 1992-1993; general counsel, 1991-1992; chief assistant state attorney, 1986-1991; other State Attorney's Office positions, 1986-1991.

Net worth: $273,267.

Campaign Slogan: "A fresh start for Jacksonville."

Favorite Book: The Bible, because he said it is comforting to him and he said he always finds something new in it.

Heroes/Role Models: His parents. Delaney said Jim and Mary Anne Delaney are just good people. He said raising kids is tough and his parents did a good job.

Jake Godbold

Age: 60.

Family: Married with one son and one grandchild.

Education: B.S. in business administration from University of North Florida.

Occupation: Owner-operator, Gateway Chemicals.

Military Experience: U.S. Army, Korean War veteran.

Government Experience: City Council, 1967-1979 (City Council president twice); mayor 1979-1986.

Net Worth: $545,031.

Campaign Slogan: "I Can Get it Done."

Favorite Book: *One Brief Shining Moment* by William Manchester. Godbold said it was very inspiring.

Heroes/Role Models: Godbold said he admires his father because he was a poor guy who worked hard and was wise and kind. Godbold also mentioned his coach at Jackson High School, Mike Howsier, because he was a strict disciplinarian and well-respected.

APPENDIX C
TEXT OF THE COMMERCIAL USED AS STIMULUS

Text of Jake Godbold's television ad:

Announcer:
It's sad, John Delaney's negative attacks distort the facts . . .

Woman's voice:
. . . added 2,000 bureaucrats . . .

Announcer:
Jake Godbold actually cut 600 city workers. But John Delaney distorts even more by trying to hide his own record. See for yourself . . .

John Delaney:
We need a new Jacksonville, we need a new fresh start.

Announcer:
Actually, John Delaney has been Ed Austin's assistant for 15 years, taken 25 pay raises. His $120,000 salary is more than even the mayor makes.

John Delaney:
As chief assistant state attorney, I've sent thousands of criminals to prison.

Announcer:
Delaney worked as assistant state attorney while 82 percent of homicide cases were plea bargained. 82 percent . . . plea bargained.

John Delaney:
And whenever I've run a department or division, we have managed it tightly . . .

Announcer:
As city attorney, Delaney gave away contracts to friends and increased his own budget by $1.4 million. John Delaney. First a negative campaign. Now not even telling us the truth about himself.

144

4B   *Jacksonville Gazette, Thurs*

Political Ad Check

By JANE SHELLY
Gazette Staff

Candidate: Jake Godbold
Race: Mayor's
Type of ad: 60-second television commercial
Date aired: Began airing Wednesday
What it says:

The ad criticizes John Delaney for distorting his record. "John Delaney. First a negative campaign, now not even telling us the truth about himself." The ad shows Delaney talking about his tight management style then counters that Delaney increased his budget as city attorney by $1.4 million.

The ad also points out that Delaney has accepted 25 pay raises as general counsel and his $120,000 salary as city is more than the

mayor makes. The spot also attacks Delaney's assertion that he's sent thousands of criminals to prison. "Delaney worked as assistant state attorney while 82 percent of homicide cases were plea bargained," the ad says.
What's the truth?:

The $1.4 million increase in the general counsel's budget represented a 3.5 percent increase. During the same period, the budgets of other city departments increased an average of 7.9 percent, indicating that Delaney held costs in check better than other officials.

The percentage quoted in the ad for plea bargains is correct. But the national average for plea bargains is 91 percent; Florida's 82 percent is the third lowest in the nation.

Delaney's $120,000 salary is consistent with what general counsels for other cities the same size as Jacksonville are paid.

Florida State student's trial begins

By ADAM YEOMANS
Associated Press Writer

TALLAHASSEE —
A university student shot and paralyzed after a minor traffic dispute is one of the witnesses being called to testify

against his accused assailant, who went on trial Tuesday.

Steven Schultz, 25, was shot after he pulled in front of another car along a busy thoroughfare lined with bars and restaurants

near the Florida State University campus in October 1994.

The street was bumper-to-bumper with students celebrating homecoming for nearby Florida A&M.

"What began as a day

W

m

The As

L
have nc
idea wl
ing or
Suwan:
Jacksor

T
about 1
Christ
Hollbr
home
Pensa
Hollbr

Be

The As.

S.
beached
got itsel
when i
trucked
rine rec

Tl
- about
weighin,
- beache
Sapelo Is

5B   *Jacksonville Gazette, Thur*

Political Ad Check

By JANE SHELLY
Gazette Staff

Candidate: Jake Godbold
Race: Mayor's
Type of ad: 60-second television commercial
Date aired: Began airing Wednesday
What it says:

The ad criticizes John Delaney for distorting his record. "John Delaney. First a negative campaign, now not even telling us the truth about himself." The ad shows Delaney talking about his tight management style then counters that Delaney increased his budget as city attorney by $1.4 million.

The ad also points out that Delaney has accepted 25 pay raises as general counsel and his $120,000 salary as city is more than the mayor makes. The spot also attacks Delaney's assertion that he's sent thousands of criminals to prison. "Delaney worked as assistant state attorney while 82 percent of homicide cases were plea bargained," the ad says.

What's the truth?:

While Delaney did increase the general counsel's budget by $1.4 million, the department's budget is such a small amount of the entire city budget that increases don't really register on Jacksonville's finances.

The percentage quoted for plea bargains is correct. But more than 75 percent of the decisions about plea bargains were made by the state attorney; the assistant state attorney has little say in plea bargains .

Delaney did accept 25 pay raises. But while Delaney is paid more than the mayor, he is paid $10,000 less than the governor of Florida.

Florida State student's trial begins

By ADAM YEOMANS
Associated Press Writer

TALLAHASSEE —
A university student shot and paralyzed after a minor traffic dispute is one of the witnesses being called to testify against his accused assailant, who went on trial Tuesday.

Steven Schultz, 25, was shot after he pulled in front of another car along a busy thoroughfare lined with bars and restaurants near the Florida State University campus in October 1994.

The street was bumper-to-bumper with students celebrating homecoming for nearby Florida A&M.

"What began as a day

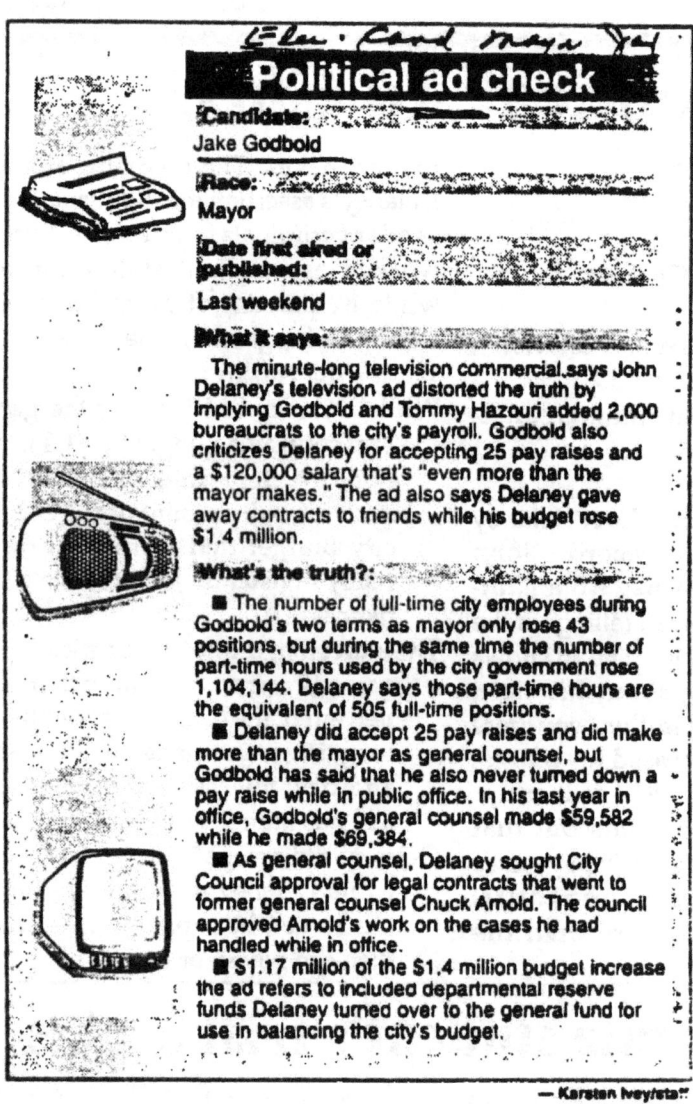

Political ad check

Candidate:

Jake Godbold

Race:

Mayor

Date first aired or published:

Last weekend

What it says:

The minute-long television commercial says John Delaney's television ad distorted the truth by implying Godbold and Tommy Hazouri added 2,000 bureaucrats to the city's payroll. Godbold also criticizes Delaney for accepting 25 pay raises and a $120,000 salary that's "even more than the mayor makes." The ad also says Delaney gave away contracts to friends while his budget rose $1.4 million.

What's the truth?:

■ The number of full-time city employees during Godbold's two terms as mayor only rose 43 positions, but during the same time the number of part-time hours used by the city government rose 1,104,144. Delaney says those part-time hours are the equivalent of 505 full-time positions.

■ Delaney did accept 25 pay raises and did make more than the mayor as general counsel, but Godbold has said that he also never turned down a pay raise while in public office. In his last year in office, Godbold's general counsel made $59,582 while he made $69,384.

■ As general counsel, Delaney sought City Council approval for legal contracts that went to former general counsel Chuck Arnold. The council approved Arnold's work on the cases he had handled while in office.

■ $1.17 million of the $1.4 million budget increase the ad refers to included departmental reserve funds Delaney turned over to the general fund for use in balancing the city's budget.

— Karsten Ivey/staff

Political Advertising

Thank you for participating in this study of political advertising. Before we begin, we'd like to get some information about you. First, we need an ID number.

Please enter the LAST four digits of your Social Security number: ☐ ☐ ☐ ☐

Now please enter your FIRST and MIDDLE initials: ☐ ☐

What is your major? ☐ Advertising   ☐ Journalism
 ☐ Telecommunications   ☐ Public Relations
 ☐ Other

Are you: ☐ Male OR ☐ Female ?

What is your age? _____

Which best describes your political views: ☐ Very Liberal   ☐ Moderate Conservative
 ☐ Liberal   ☐ Conservative
 ☐ Moderate Liberal   ☐ Very Conservative
 ☐ Middle of the Road

Which party do you most often vote for? ☐ Democrat   ☐ Independent
 ☐ Republican   ☐ Other

Please think about newspapers that you are familiar with. Now check the box in each line below that describes how you think those newspapers rate. Boxes "1" and "7" indicate very strong feelings; boxes "2" and "6" indicate strong feelings; boxes "3" and "5" represent fairly weak feelings; and box "4" indicates that you are undecided.

Most newspapers:	1	2	3	4	5	6	7	
Are unfair	☐	☐	☐	☐	☐	☐	☐	Are fair
Are biased	☐	☐	☐	☐	☐	☐	☐	Are unbiased
Don't tell the whole story	☐	☐	☐	☐	☐	☐	☐	Tell the whole story
Are inaccurate	☐	☐	☐	☐	☐	☐	☐	Are accurate
Do not separate fact and opinion	☐	☐	☐	☐	☐	☐	☐	Separate fact and opinion
Have poorly trained reporters	☐	☐	☐	☐	☐	☐	☐	Have well trained reporters
Are liberal	☐	☐	☐	☐	☐	☐	☐	Are conservative
Support Democrats	☐	☐	☐	☐	☐	☐	☐	Support Republicans

Please respond to the following statements:
Check the box that best describes you.

	Very strongly disagree	Strongly disagree	Disagree	Neither agree nor disagree	Agree	Strongly agree	Very strongly agree
I like tasks that require little thought once I've learned them.	❑	❑	❑	❑	❑	❑	❑
I prefer to think about small daily projects instead of long-term projects.	❑	❑	❑	❑	❑	❑	❑
I really enjoy a task that involves coming up with new solutions and problems.	❑	❑	❑	❑	❑	❑	❑
I don't like to have the responsibility of handling situations that require a lot of thinking.	❑	❑	❑	❑	❑	❑	❑
The idea of relying on thought to make my way to the top does not appeal to me.	❑	❑	❑	❑	❑	❑	❑
I prefer complex problems to simple problems.	❑	❑	❑	❑	❑	❑	❑
I think only as hard as I have to.	❑	❑	❑	❑	❑	❑	❑
I prefer to just let things happen rather than trying to understand why they turned out that way.	❑	❑	❑	❑	❑	❑	❑
The notion of thinking abstractly is not appealing to me.	❑	❑	❑	❑	❑	❑	❑
I would rather do something that requires little thought than something that challenges my thinking abilities.	❑	❑	❑	❑	❑	❑	❑
Thinking is not my idea of fun.	❑	❑	❑	❑	❑	❑	❑
I find satisfaction in deliberating hard and for long hours.	❑	❑	❑	❑	❑	❑	❑
I prefer my life to be filled with puzzles that I must solve.	❑	❑	❑	❑	❑	❑	❑
I try to anticipate and avoid situations where there is a likely chance that I will have to think in depth.	❑	❑	❑	❑	❑	❑	❑
Simply knowing the answer rather than understanding the reasons for the answer to a problem is fine with me.	❑	❑	❑	❑	❑	❑	❑

For the following statements, check the box that best describes how often you:

Talk with my friends or family about politics.

Never	Rarely	Sometimes	Often	Always
☐	☐	☐	☐	☐

Vote in elections in which I am an eligible voter.

Never	Rarely	Sometimes	Often	Always
☐	☐	☐	☐	☐

Work for a campaign by doing things like distributing information or making phone calls.

Never	Rarely	Sometimes	Often	Always
☐	☐	☐	☐	☐

Contribute money to a candidate's campaign.

Never	Rarely	Sometimes	Often	Always
☐	☐	☐	☐	☐

Wear a button or put a bumper sticker on my car showing my support of a candidate.

Never	Rarely	Sometimes	Often	Always
☐	☐	☐	☐	☐

Write a lawmaker to express my views on an issue.

Never	Rarely	Sometimes	Often	Always
☐	☐	☐	☐	☐

Watch television news about politics.

Never	Rarely	Sometimes	Often	Always
☐	☐	☐	☐	☐

Watch political debates.

Never	Rarely	Sometimes	Often	Always
☐	☐	☐	☐	☐

Read a political stories in a newspaper or magazine.

Never	Rarely	Sometimes	Often	Always
☐	☐	☐	☐	☐

Attend political rallies or events.

Never	Rarely	Sometimes	Often	Always
☐	☐	☐	☐	☐

Pay attention to political advertising on TV

Never	Rarely	Sometimes	Often	Always
☐	☐	☐	☐	☐

Are you ☐ registered to vote   OR   ☐ not registered to vote?

The Election:

This section gives you background on the election for which the political commercial has been created. Please read this information carefully.

Jacksonville residents will soon be seeking a new mayor. The current mayor, Ed Austin, has decided not to run again and will retire at the end of his term. After a series of primaries, two candidates were chosen to go head to head in the general election this spring. The candidates are:

John Delaney	_Jake Godbold_
Age: 38.	*Age:* 60.
Family: Married with two daughters and one son.	*Family:* Married with one son and one grandchild.
Education: J.D. from Stetson University, B.A. in history from the University of North Florida.	*Education:* B.S. in business administration from University of North Florida.
Occupation: Attorney.	*Occupation:* Owner-operator, Gateway Chemicals.
Military Experience: None.	*Military Experience:* U.S. Army, Korean War veteran.
Government Experience: General counsel, 1993-1994; chief of staff, Mayor's Office, 1992-1993; general counsel, 1991-1992; chief assistant state attorney, 1986-1991; other State Attorney's Office positions, 1986-1991.	*Government Experience:* City Council, 1967-1979 (City Council president twice); mayor 1979-1986.
Net worth: $273,267.	*Net Worth:* $545,031.
Campaign Slogan: "A fresh start for Jacksonville."	*Campaign Slogan:* "I Can Get it Done."
Favorite Book: The Bible, because he said it is comforting to him and he said he always finds something new in it.	*Favorite Book:* One Brief Shining Moment by William Manchester. Godbold said it was very inspiring.
Heroes/Role Models: His parents. Delaney said Jim and Mary Anne Delaney are just good people. He said raising kids is tough and his parents did a good job.	*Heroes/Role Models:* Godbold said he admires his father because he was a poor guy who worked hard and was wise and kind. Godbold also mentioned his coach at Jackson High School, Mike Howsier, because he was a strict disciplinarian and well-respected.

STOP!

Wait here until everyone has finished. In a minute you will see an ad that Jake Godbold ran in response to claims made by John Delaney.
DO NOT TURN THE PAGE UNTIL YOU HAVE SEEN THE AD.

Reviewing the Ad

After the ad you just saw was broadcast, the local newspaper printed the following story reviewing the claims made in the Jake Godbold ad. The information was compiled by a reporter at the paper.

Please read the information carefully.

6B   *Jacksonville Gazette, Thursday, February 15, 1996*

Political Ad Check

By JANE SHELLY
Gazette Staff

Candidate: Jake Godbold
Race: Mayor's
Type of ad: 60-second television commercial
Date aired: Began airing Wednesday
What it says:

The ad criticizes John Delaney for distorting his record. "John Delaney. First a negative campaign, now not even telling us the truth about himself." The ad shows Delaney talking about his tight management style then counters that Delaney increased his budget as city attorney by $1.4 million.

The ad also points out that Delaney has accepted 25 pay raises as general counsel and his $120,000 salary as city is more than the mayor makes. The spot also attacks Delaney's assertion that he's sent thousands of criminals to prison. "Delaney worked as assistant state attorney while 82 percent of homicide cases were plea bargained," the ad says.

What's the truth?:

The $1.4 million increase in the general counsel's budget represented a 3.5 percent increase. During the same period, the budgets of other city departments increased an average of 7.9 percent, indicating that Delaney held costs in check better than other officials.

The percentage quoted in the ad for plea bargains is correct. But the national average for plea bargains is 91 percent; Florida's 82 percent is the third lowest in the nation.

Delaney's $120,000 salary is consistent with what general counsels for other cities the same size as Jacksonville are paid.

Florida State student's trial begins

By ADAM YEOMANS
Associated Press Writer

TALLAHASSEE — A university student shot and paralyzed after a minor traffic dispute is one of the wit- against his accused assailant, who went on trial Tuesday.

Steven Schultz, 25, was shot after he pulled in front of another car along a busy thoroughfare lined with bars and restaurants near the Florida State University campus in October 1994.

The street was bumper-to-bumper with students celebrating homecoming for nearby Florida A&M.

"What began as a dis-

Woman, 19 mystery I-1

The Associated Press

LIVE OAK — Police have no suspects and have no idea what prompted a shooting on Interstate 10 in Suwannee County that left a Jacksonville woman dead.

The shooting came at about 12:30 a.m. Tuesday as Christopher and Dana Hollbrook where driving home to Jacksonville from Pensacola. Christopher Hollbrook, stationed at Jack-

sonville Nav has been Pensacola, spent the w for an apartr

About Live Oak, tw in a white f with a black the interstate fired twice a car, police st

A bull Hollbrook, 1 Hollbrook w dead at ab

Beached whale se

The Associated Press

SAVANNAH, Ga. — A beached pygmy killer whale got itself a Florida vacation when it was rescued and trucked Wednesday to a marine recovery tank.

The small, gray whale - about seven feet long and weighing about 250 pounds - beached itself Saturday on Sapelo Island, said Mike Har-

ris, a wildlif the Georgia Natural Reso

The wh into a boat, l mainland an truck to Mai Augustine, th ity with a tar whale could care, Harris :

He saic recovering.

Pygmy

Now we'd like to know your opinion about the commercial you just saw.

Check one box on each line below that describes how you think the ad rates. Boxes "1" and "7" indicate very strong feelings; boxes "2" and "6" indicate strong feelings; boxes "3" and "5" represent fairly weak feelings; and box "4" indicates that you are undecided.

The commercial is:

	1	2	3	4	5	6	7	
Unbelievable	☐	☐	☐	☐	☐	☐	☐	Believable
Untrustworthy	☐	☐	☐	☐	☐	☐	☐	Trustworthy
Not convincing	☐	☐	☐	☐	☐	☐	☐	Convincing
Not credible	☐	☐	☐	☐	☐	☐	☐	Credible
Unreasonable	☐	☐	☐	☐	☐	☐	☐	Reasonable
Deceptive	☐	☐	☐	☐	☐	☐	☐	Truthful
Questionable	☐	☐	☐	☐	☐	☐	☐	Unquestionable
Inconclusive	☐	☐	☐	☐	☐	☐	☐	Conclusive
Unethical	☐	☐	☐	☐	☐	☐	☐	Ethical
Inaccurate	☐	☐	☐	☐	☐	☐	☐	Accurate

Based on the information you've received today, what is your opinion of the candidate who sponsored the ad, Jake Godbold? Check the box in each line that best represents your views.

	1	2	3	4	5	6	7	
Incompetent	☐	☐	☐	☐	☐	☐	☐	Competent
Weak	☐	☐	☐	☐	☐	☐	☐	Strong
Dumb	☐	☐	☐	☐	☐	☐	☐	Smart
Unqualified	☐	☐	☐	☐	☐	☐	☐	Qualified
Cannot be trusted	☐	☐	☐	☐	☐	☐	☐	Can be trusted
Unethical	☐	☐	☐	☐	☐	☐	☐	Ethical
Unfriendly	☐	☐	☐	☐	☐	☐	☐	Friendly
Irrational	☐	☐	☐	☐	☐	☐	☐	Rational
Unappealing	☐	☐	☐	☐	☐	☐	☐	Appealing
Inexperienced	☐	☐	☐	☐	☐	☐	☐	Experienced

A few final questions about the television commercial you just saw:

When you were reading the newspaper story about the Godbold commercial, what were you thinking about the commercial and the story? *Please write out as much as you can think of. Use the back of this sheet if you need more space.*

_____

_____

_____

_____

_____

_____

If the election were held tomorrow and you were eligible to vote, which statement best describes how you would vote? *Check one box only*

☐ Would definitely vote for John Delaney

☐ Would probably vote for John Delaney

☐ Still undecided: Support John Delaney and Jake Godbold equally.

☐ Would probably vote for Jake Godbold

☐ Would definitely vote for Jake Godbold

☐ I would not vote in this election.

Which information *most* helped you decide how to vote in the election? *Check one box only*

☐ Biographical information about the candidates in the box

☐ Information contained in Godbold's television commercial

☐ Information contained in the newspaper story about the ad

☐ Information provided about the newspaper's objectivity

Please explain why you chose to vote the way you indicated above:

_____

_____

_____

_____

Had you heard of John Delaney OR Jake Godbold before participating in this study today?

No ☐

Yes ☐

If **YES**, what was your opinion of the candidates?

	Liked Very Much	Liked	No Opinion	Disliked	Disliked Very Much
John Delaney:	☐	☐	☐	☐	☐
Jake Godbold:	☐	☐	☐	☐	☐

Please think back to the information you were given in the newspaper article about the Godbold commercial.

Based on information that you were given about the newspaper's objectivity, would you say the newspaper would be likely to: (check one box)

☐ Support Godbold ☐ Be neutral ☐ Support John Delaney

The arguments presented in the newspaper article to refute Jake Godbold's claims were: *Check one box in each row.*

	1	2	3	4	5	6	7	
Weak	☐	☐	☐	☐	☐	☐		Strong
Unconvincing	☐	☐	☐	☐	☐	☐	☐	Convincing
Irrational	☐	☐	☐	☐	☐	☐	☐	Rational
Not believable	☐	☐	☐	☐	☐	☐	☐	Believable

How useful was the newspaper article about the ad in helping you evaluate the candidates?

☐ Very useful ☐ Somewhat useful ☐ Not useful at all

How likely would you be to read this type of article in the newspaper during an election campaign?

☐ Very likely ☐ Somewhat likely ☐ Not at all likely

Thank you very much for your participation in this study. Please take your form to one of the administrators to be turned in. The administrator will check to make sure you filled in all of the requested information, then add your name to the extra-credit list for your instructor.

Subjects in the no-adwatch control were presented with the following information instead of an adwatch. The information was presented in the same format as the newspaper page shown to other subjects.

Editor's note: As part of the Gazette's election coverage, we periodically publish the text of political commercials.

Candidate: Jake Godbold
Race: Mayor's
Type of ad: 30-second television commercial
Date aired: Began airing Wednesday
Text of the ad:

Announcer: It's sad. John Delaney's negative attacks distort the facts...

Woman's voice: ...added 2,000 bureaucrats...

Announcer: Jake Godbold actually cut 600 city workers. But John Delaney distorts even more by trying to hide his own record. See for yourself.

John Delaney: "We need a new Jacksonville, we need a new fresh start."

Announcer: Actually, John Delaney has been Ed Austin's assistant for 15 years, taken 25 pay raises. His $120,000 salary is more than even the mayor makes.

John Delaney: "As chief assistant state attorney, I've sent thousands of criminals to prison."

Announcer: Delaney worked as assistant state attorney while 82 percent of homicide cases were plea bargained. 82 percent ... plea bargained.

John Delaney: "And whenever I've run a department or division, we have managed it tightly..."

Announcer: As city attorney, Delaney gave away contracts to friends and increased his own budget by $1.4 million. John Delaney. First a negative campaign, now not even telling us the truth about himself.

REFERENCES

Ahlering, R. F. (1987). Need for cognition, attitudes, and the 1984 presidential election. Journal of Research in Personality, 21, 100-102.

Ailes, R. (1991, January/February). TV-spot critics: "Boring and biased." Washington Journalism Review, p. 27.

Alger, D. E. (1994, October). The media, the public and the development of candidates' images in the 1992 presidential election. Research paper R-14 from the Joan Shorenstein Center, Harvard University.

Alger, D. E., Kern, M., & West, D. M. (1993, May). Political advertising: The information environment and the voter in the 1992 presidential election. Paper presented at annual meeting of the International Communication Association, Washington, DC.

Alter, J. (1990, October 29). The media mud squad. Newsweek, p. 37.

Alwitt, L. F, & Mitchell, A. A. (1985). Psychological Processes and Advertising Effects: Theory, Research and Application. Hillsdale, NJ: Lawrence Erlbaum Associates.

Ansolabehere, S., Iyengar, S., Simon, A., & Valentino, N. (1994). Does attack advertising demobilize the electorate? American Political Science Review, 88, 829-838.

Ansolabehere, S., & Iyengar, S. (1995). Going Negative: How Attack Ads Shrink and Polarize the Electorate. New York: Free Press.

Areni, C. S. (1991). Differential effects of comparative advertising for an unfamiliar brand: The moderating role of audience elaboration. Doctoral dissertation, University of Florida.

Beltramini, R. F. (1982). Advertising Perceived Believability Scale. In D. R. Corrigan, F. B. Kraft, and R. H. Ross (Eds.), Proceedings of the Southwestern Marketing Association. (pp. 1-3). Wichita, KS: Southwestern Marketing Association, Wichita State University.

157

Beltramini, R. F. (1988). Perceived believability of warning label information presented in cigarette advertising. Journal of Advertising, 17(1), 26-32.

Bennett, S. E. (1989). Trends in Americans' political information, 1967-1987. American Politics Quarterly, 17, 422-435.

Boot, W. (1989, January/February). Campaign `88: T.V. overdoses on the inside dope. Columbia Journalism Review, 27, 23-29.

Bowers, T. A. (1975). The coverage of political advertising by the prestige press in 1972. Mass Communication Review, 2, 19-24.

Broder, D. (1989, January 19). Should news media police the accuracy of ads? Washington Post, p. A22.

Burnkrant, R. E., & Sawyer, A. G. (1983). Effects on involvement and message content on information processing intensity. In R. Harris (Ed.), Information Processing Research in Advertising. (pp. 43-65). Hillsdale, NJ: Lawrence Erlbaum and Associates.

Cacioppo, J. T., & Petty, R. E. (1979). Effects of message repetition and position on cognitive response, recall, and persuasion. Journal of Personality and Social Psychology, 37, 97-109.

Cacioppo, J. T., & Petty, R. E. (1982). The need for cognition. Journal of Personality and Social Psychology, 42, 116-131.

Cacioppo, J. T., & Petty, R. E. (1984). The need for cognition: Relationship to attitudinal processes. In R. McGlynn, J. Maddux, C. Stoltenberg, & J. Harvey (Eds.), Social Perception in Clinical and Counseling Psychology. (pp. 113-139). Lubbock, TX: Texas Tech University Press.

Cacioppo, J. T., & Petty, R. E. (1985). Central and peripheral routes to persuasion: The role of message repetition. In L. F. Alwitt & A. A. Mitchell (Eds.), Psychological Processes and Advertising Effects: Theory, Research and Application. (pp. 91-111). Hillsdale, NJ: Lawrence Erlbaum Associates.

Cacioppo, J. T., Petty, R. E., Feinstein, J. A., & Jarvis, W. B. G. (1996). Dispositional differences in cognitive motivation: The life and times of individuals varying in need for cognition. Psychological Bulletin, 119, 197-253.

Cacioppo, J. T., Petty, R. E., & Kao, C. F. (1984). The efficient assessment of need for cognition. Journal of Personality Assessment, 48, 306-307.

Cacioppo, J. T., Petty, R. E., Kao, C. F., & Rodriguez, R. (1986). Central and peripheral routes to persuasion: An individual difference perspective. Journal of Personality and Social Psychology, 51, 1032-1043.

Cacioppo, J. T., & Petty, R. E., & Morris, K. (1983). Effects of need for cognition on message evaluation, recall and persuasion. Journal of Personality and Social Psychology, 45, 805-818.

Cacioppo, J. T., Petty, R. E., & Stoltenberg, C. (1985). Processes of social influence: The Elaboration Likelihood Model of persuasion. In P. Kendall (Ed.), Advances in Cognitive Behavioral Research and Therapy: Vol. 4. New York: Academic Press.

Campbell, A., Converse, P. E., Miller, W. E., and Stokes, D. E. (1960). The American Voter. Chicago: University of Chicago Press.

Campbell, D. T., & Stanley, J. C. (1968). Experimental and Quasi-Experimental Designs for Research (3rd printing). Chicago: Rand McNally.

Canellos, P. S. (1996, February. 26.). Media critic decries coverage of N.H. campaign: Is reporting usurped by analysis? The Boston Globe, p. 7.

Cappella, J. N., & Jamieson, K. H. (1994). Broadcast adwatch effects: A field experiment. Communication Research, 21, 342-365.

Chaiken, S. (1980). Heuristic versus systematic information processing and the use of source versus message cues in persuasion. Journal of Personality and Social Psychology, 39, 752-766.

Cialdini, R. B., Levy, A., Herman, P., Kozlowski, L., & Petty R. E. (1976). Elastic shifts of opinion: Determinants of direction and durability. Journal of Personality and Social Psychology, 34, 663-672.

Cialdini, R. B., Petty, R. E., & Cacioppo, J. T. (1981). Attitude and attitude change. In M. Rosenzweig & L. Porter (Eds.), Annual Review of Psychology Vol. 32. Palo Alto, CA: Annual Reviews.

Clark, E. (1988). The Want Makers: Inside the World of Advertising. New York: Penguin Books.

Cohen, A. R., Stotland, E., & Wolfe, D. M. (1955). An experimental investigation of need for cognition. Journal of Abnormal and Social Psychology, 51, 291-294.

Condra, M. B. (1992). The link between need for cognition and political interest, involvement, and media usage. Psychology: A Journal of Human Behavior, 29, 13-18.

Cook, T. D., & Campbell, D. T. (1979). Quasi-Experimentation: Design & Analysis Issues for Field Settings. Boston: Houghton Mifflin.

Cronbach, L. J. (1951). Coefficient alpha and the internal structure of tests. Psychometrika, 16, 279-334.

Devlin, L. P. (1993). Contrasts in presidential campaign commercials of 1992. American Behavioral Scientist, 37, 272-290.

Devlin, L. P. (1995). Political commercials in American presidential elections. In L. L. Kaid & C. Holtz-Bacha (Eds.), Political Advertising in Western Democracies: Parties and Candidates on Television. (pp. 186-205). Thousand Oaks, CA: Sage.

Drew, E. (1989). Election Journal: Political Events of 1987-1988. New York: William Morrow.

Eagly, A. H., & Manis, M. (1966). Evaluation of message and communication as a function of involvement. Journal of Personality and Social Psychology, 3, 483-485.

Fallows, J. (1996). Breaking the News: How the Media Undermine American Democracy. New York: Pantheon Books.

Ferguson, M., Chung, M., & Weigold, M. (1985, May). Need for cognition and the medium dependency components of reliance and exposure. Paper presented a the meeting of the International Communication Association, Honolulu, HI.

Fishbein, M., & Ajzen, I. (1981). Acceptance, yielding, and impact: Cognitive Processes in Persuasion. In R. E. Petty, T. Ostrom, & T. C. Brock (Eds.), Cognitive Responses to Persuasion. (pp. 339-359). Hillsdale, NJ: Lawrence Erlbaum.

Garfield, B. (1990, Nov. 5). Let voters take warning: Political advertising in this country is a travesty. Advertising Age, pp. 28-29.

Garramone, G. M. (1984). Voter responses to negative political ads. Journalism Quarterly, 61, 250-259.

Garramone, G. M. (1985). Effects of negative political advertising: The roles of sponsor and rebuttal. Journal of Broadcasting and Electronic Media, 29, 147-159.

Garramone, G. M., Atkin, C. K., Pinkleton, B. E., & Cole, R. T. (1990). Effects of negative advertising on the political process. Journal of Broadcasting and Electronic Media, 34, 299-311.

Garramone, G. M., & Smith, S. J. (1984). Reactions to political advertising: Clarifying sponsor effects. Journalism Quarterly, 61, 771-775.

Gazinao, C., & McGrath, K. (1986). Measuring the concept of credibility. Journalism Quarterly, 63, 451-462.

Geiger, S. (1993, May). Truth in political advertising: The effects of ad watch articles on the evaluation and memory for political candidates. Presented to the annual meeting of the International Communication Association, Washington, DC.

Goodman, E. (1990, October 23). Two political negatives don't make a positive. Newsday, p. 52.

Gronbeck, B. E. (1992). Negative narratives in 1988 presidential campaign ads. Quarterly Journal of Speech, 78, 333-346.

Hagstrom, J., & Guskind, R. (1992, November 5). In the gutter. National Journal, pp. 2477-2482.

Hernandez, D. G. (1996, February 24). Covering election campaigns. Editor and Publisher, p. 12

Hinerfeld, D. S. (1990, May). How political ads subtract. Washington Monthly, pp. 12-22.

Hovland, C. I., Janis, I. L, & Kelley, H. H. (1953). Communication and Persuasion: Psychological Studies of Opinion Change. New Haven, CT: Yale University Press.

Hovland, C. I, & Mandell, W. (1952). An experimental comparison of conclusion-drawing by the communicator and the audience. Journal of Abnormal and Social Psychology, 47, 581-588.

Hovland, C. I., & Weiss, W. (1951). The influence of source credibility on communication effectiveness. Public Opinion Quarterly, 15, 635-650.

Hume, E. (1991). Restoring the Bond: Connecting Campaign Coverage to Voters: A Report of the Campaign Lessons for '92 Project. Cambridge, MA: Harvard University.

Jacobson, G. C. (1987). The Politics of Congressional Elections (2nd ed.). Glenview, IL: Scott, Foresman and Company.

Jamieson, K. H. (1992a). Dirty Politics: Deception, Distraction, Democracy. New York: Oxford University Press.

Jamieson, K. H. (1992b). Packaging The Presidency: A History and Criticism of Presidential Campaign Advertising. New York: Oxford University Press.

Jamieson, K. H., & Campbell, K. K. (1992). The Interplay of Influence: News, Advertising, Politics, and the Mass Media (3rd ed.). Belmont, CA: Wadsworth Publishing.

Jeffres, L. W. (1986). Mass Media Processes and Effects. Prospect Heights, IL: Waveland Press.

Johnson-Cartee, K. S., & Copeland, G. A. (1989). Southern voter's reaction to negative political ads in the 1986 election. Journalism Quarterly, 66, 888-893.

Joslyn, R. A. (1990). Election campaigns as occasions for civic education. In D. L. Swanson & D. Nimmo (Eds.), New Directions in Political Communication: A Resource Book. (pp. 86-119). Newbury Park, CA: Sage.

Just, M., Crigler, A., & Wallach, L. (1990). Thirty seconds or thirty minutes: What viewers learn from spot advertisements and candidate debates. Journal of Communication, 40, 120-133.

Kaid, L. L. (1981). Political advertising. In D. D. Nimmo & K. R. Sanders (Eds.), Handbook of Political Communication. (pp. 249-271). Beverly Hills, CA: Sage.

Kaid, L. L., Gobetz, R. H., Garner, J., Leland, C. M., & Scott, D. K. (1993). Television news and presidential campaigns: The legitimization of televised political advertising. Social Science Quarterly, 74, 274-285.

Kaid, L. L., & Johnston, A. (1991). Negative versus positive television advertising in U.S. presidential campaigns, 1960-1988. Journal of Communication, 41, 53-64.

Kaid, L. L., McKinnon, L. M., Tedesco, J. C. (1995, May). Televised advertising as nightly news: A content analysis of adwatches from the 1992 presidential campaign. Paper presented at the annual meeting of the International Communications Association, Albuquerque, NM.

Kanouse, D. E. (1984). Explaining negativity biases in evaluation and choice behavior: Theory and research. In T. C. Kinnear (Ed.), Advances in Consumer Research. (pp. 703-707).

Kern, M. (1989). <u>30-Second Politics: Political Advertising in the 1980s</u>. New York: Praeger.

Kern, M., West, D., Alger, D. E. (1993, September). <u>Political advertising, ad watches and televised news in the 1992 presidential election</u>. Paper presented at the annual meeting of the American Political Science Association, Washington, DC.

Kessel, J. H. (1988). <u>Presidential Campaign Politics: Coalition Strategies and Citizen Response</u> (3rd ed.). Chicago: The Dorsey Press.

Lassiter, G. D., Briggs, M. A., Shaw, R. D. (1991). Need for cognition, causal processing, and memory for behavior. <u>Personality and Social Psychology Bulletin, 17</u>, 694-700.

Lasswell, H. D. (1927). Propaganda. In E. R. A. Sligeman & A. Johnson (Eds.), <u>Encyclopedia of the Social Sciences (Vol. 12)</u>. 521-528.

Lichter, S. R., & Noyles, R. E. (1995). <u>Good Intentions Make Bad News: Why Americans Hate Campaign Journalism</u>. Lanham, MD: Rowman & Littlefield Publishers, Inc.

MacInnis, D. J., & Jaworski, B. J. (1989). Information processing from advertisements: Toward an integrative framework. <u>Journal of Marketing, 53</u>, 1-23.

Manheim, J. B., & Rich, R. C. (1991). <u>Empirical Political Analysis: Research Methods in Political Science</u>. New York: Longman.

Martinelli, K. A., & Chaffee, S. H. (1995). Measuring new-voter learning via three channels of political information. <u>Journalism & Mass Communication Quarterly, 72</u>, 18-32.

McClure, R. D., & Patterson, T. E. (1974). Television news and political advertising: The impact of exposure on voter beliefs. <u>Communication Research, 1</u>, 3-31.

McGuire, W. J. (1969). The nature of attitudes and attitude change. In G. Lindzey & E. Aronson (Eds.), <u>The Handbook of Social Psychology: Vol 3</u>. (pp. 136-314). Reading MA: Addison Wesley. 136-314.

McGuire, W. J. (1989). Theoretical foundations of campaigns. In R. E. Rice & C. K. Atkins (Eds.), <u>Public Communication Campaigns</u> (2nd Ed.). (pp. 43-65). Beverly Hills, CA: Sage.

McKinnon, L. M., Kaid, L. L, Murphy, J., & Acree, C. K. (1996). Policing political ads: An analysis of five leading newspaper' responses to 1992 political advertisements. Journalism and Mass Communication Quarterly, 73, 66-76.

Meadow, R. G. (1989). Political campaigns. In R. E. Rice & C. K. Atkins (Eds.), Public Communication Campaigns (2nd Ed.). (pp. 253-272) Beverly Hills, CA: Sage.

Media Scoreboard, Round Three: Experts assess Campaign '92 coverage (a panel discussion). (1992). The Homestretch: New Politics. New Media. New Voters? New York: The Freedom Forum Media Studies Center. pp. 83-98.

Merritt, S. (1984). Negative political advertising: Some empirical findings. Journal of Advertising, 13(3), 27-38.

Meyer, P. (1988). Defining and measuring credibility of newspapers: Developing an index. Journalism Quarterly, 65, 567-574, 588.

Mickelson, S. (1989). From Whistle Stop to Sound Bite: Four Decades of Politics and Television. New York: Praeger.

Milburn, M. A. (1991). Persuasion and Politics: The Social Psychology of Public Opinion. Pacific Grove, CA: Brooks/Cole Publishing.

Milburn, M. A., & Brown, J. (1995). Busted by the Ad Police: Journalists' Coverage of Political Campaign Ads in the 1992 Presidential Campaign. Research paper R-15 from the Joan Shorenstein Center, Harvard University.

Mills, J., & Harvey, J. (1972). Opinion change as a function of when information about the communicator is received and whether he is attractive or expert. Journal of Personality and Social Psychology, 21, 52-55.

National Journal. (1990, October. 27). The press plays referee on campaign ads. National Journal, p. 2595.

Norman, R. (1976). When what is said is important: A comparison of expert and attractive sources. Journal of Experimental Social Psychology, 12, 294-300.

O'Sullivan, P. B., & Geiger, S. (1995). Does the watchdog bite? Newspaper ad watch articles and political attack ads. Journalism and Mass Communication Quarterly, 72, 771-785.

Osberg, T. M. (1987). The convergent and discriminant validity of the need for cognition scale. Journal of Personality Assessment, 51, 441-450.

Osgood, C. E. (1965). Cross cultural comparability of attitude measurement via multilingual semantic differentials. In I. S. Steiner & M. Fishbein (Eds.), <u>Recent Students in Social Psychology</u>. New York: Holt, Reinhard, & Winston.

Osgood, C. E., & Tannenbaum, P. H. (1955). The principle of congruity in the prediction of attitude change. <u>Psychological Review, 62</u>, 42-55.

Owen, D. (1991). <u>Mediated Messages in American Presidential Elections</u>. New York: Greenwood.

Patterson, T. E. (1993). <u>Out of Order</u>. New York: Vintage Books.

Patterson, T. E., & McClure, R. (1976). <u>The Unseeing Eye: The Myth of Television's Power in National Elections</u>. New York: G. P. Putnam.

Pease, E. C. (1992). "New" media voices challenge the "old" media status quo. <u>The Homestretch: New Politics, New Media, New Voters?</u> New York: The Freedom Forum Media Studies Center. pp. 99-101.

Perri, M., & Wolfgang, A. P. (1988). A modified measure of need for cognition. <u>Psychological Reports, 62</u>, 955-957.

Petty, R. E., & Cacioppo, J. T. (1979). Issue involvement can increase or decrease persuasion by enhancing message-relevant cognitive responses. <u>Journal of Personality and Social Psychology, 37</u>, 1915-1926.

Petty, R. E., & Cacioppo, J. T. (1980). Effects on issue involvement on attitudes in an advertising context. In G. Gorn & M. Goldberg (Eds.), <u>Proceedings of the Division 23 Program</u>. (pp. 75-79). Montreal, Canada: Division 23 of the American Psychological Association.

Petty, R. E., & Cacioppo, J. T. (1981). <u>Attitudes and persuasion: Classic and contemporary approaches</u>. Dubuque, IA: Wm. C. Brown Co. Publishers.

Petty, R. E., & Cacioppo, J. T. (1986a). <u>Communication and Persuasion: Central and Peripheral Routes to Attitude Change</u>. New York: Springer-Verlag.

Petty, R. E., & Cacioppo, J. T. (1986b). The Elaboration Likelihood Model of persuasion. In L. Berkowitz (Ed.), <u>Advances in Experimental Social Psychology: Vol. 19</u>. (pp. 123-205). New York: Academic Press.

Petty, R. E., & Cacioppo, J. T., & Goldman, R. (1981). Personal involvement as a determinant of argument-based persuasion. <u>Journal of Personality and Social Psychology, 41</u>, 847-855.

Petty, R. E., Cacioppo, J. T., & Schumann, D. (1983). Central and peripheral routes to advertising effectiveness: The moderating role of involvement. Journal of Consumer Research, 10, 134-148.

Petty, R. E., Harkins, S. G., & Williams, K. D. (1980). The effects of group diffusion of cognitive effort on attitudes: An information processing view. Journal of Personality and Social Psychology, 38, 81-92.

Petty, R. E., Kasmer, J. A., Haugtvedt, C. P., & Cacioppo, J. T. (1987). Source and message factors in persuasion: A reply to Stiff's critique of the Elaboration Likelihood Model. Communication Monographs, 54, 233-249.

Petty, R. E., Wegener, D. T., Rabrigar, L. R., Priester, J. R., & Cacioppo, J. T. (1993). Conceptual and methodological issues in the Elaboration Likelihood Model of persuasion: A reply to the Michigan State critics. Communication Theory, 3, 336-361.

Petty, R. E., Wells, G. L., & Brock, T. C. (1976). Distraction can enhance or reduce yielding to propaganda: Thought disruption verses effort justification. Journal of Personality and Social Psychology, 34, 874-884.

Pfau, M, & Burgoon, M. (1988). Inoculation in political campaign communication. Human Communication Research, 15, 91-111.

Pfau, M,. & Louden, A. (1994). Effectiveness of adwatch formats in deflecting political attack ads. Communication Research, 21, 325-341.

Pinkleton, B. E., (1993, August). The role of comparative information in political advertising evaluations and candidate evaluations. Paper presented at the annual meeting of the Association for Education in Journalism and Mass Communication, Kansas City, MO.

Priester, J., & Petty, R. E. (1995). Source attributions and persuasion: Perceived honesty as a determinant of message scrutiny. Personality and Social Psychology Bulletin, 21, 637-654.

Rachlin, S. (1992). Insider's guide to the coverage. In Covering the Presidential Primaries. (pp. 23-34). New York: The Freedom Forum Media Studies Center.

Roddy, B. L., & Garramone, G. M. (1988). Appeals and strategies of negative political advertising. Journal of Broadcasting and Electronic Media, 32, 415-427.

Rosenstiel, T. (1993). Strange Bedfellows: How Television and the Presidential Candidates Changed American Politics, 1992. New York: Hyperion.

Runkel, D. R. (1989). Campaign for President: The Managers Look at '88. Dover, MA: Auburn House.

Sadowski, C. J., & Gulgoz, S. (1992). Internal consistency and test-reliability of the Need for Cognition Scale. Perceptual and Motor Skills, 74, 610.

Perri, M., & Wolfgang, A. P. (1988). A modified measure of need for cognition. Psychological Reports, 62, 955-957.

Smith, T. J. (1990, January/February). The watchdog's bite. American Enterprise, pp. 63-70.

Squire, R. (1991, January/February). 1990 coverage: A good beginning. Washington Journalism Review, p. 26.

Stebenne, D. (1993). Media coverage of American presidential elections: A historical perspective. In The Finish Line: Covering the Campaign's Final Days. (pp. 79-91). New York: The Freedom Forum Media Studies Center.

Tanka, J. S., Panter, A. T., & Winborne, W. C. (1988). Dimensions of the need for cognition: Subscales and gender differences. Multivariate Behavioral Research, 23, 35-50.

Thorson, E., Christ, W. G., & Caywood, C. (1991). Effects of issue-image strategies, attack and support appeals, music, and visual content in political commercials. Journal of Broadcasting and Electronic Media, 35, 465-486.

Thorson, E., & Coyle, J. (1994, May). A comparison of the impact of political ads appearing in radio, newspaper and television. Paper presented at the annual meeting of the International Communication Association, Sidney, Australia.

Times Mirror Center for the People & the Press (1992). The campaign and the press at half-time. Supplement to the July/August 1992 issue of Columbia Journalism Review. pp. 1-8.

Times Mirror Center for the People & the Press (1993). The press and Campaign '92: A self-assessment. Supplement to the March/April 1993 issue of Columbia Journalism Review. pp. 1-8.

Tinkham, S. F., & Weaver-Lariscy, R. A. (1994). Ethical judgments of political television commercials as predictors of attitude toward the ad. Journal of Advertising, 23, 43-57.

Trent, J. S., & Friedenberg, R. V. (1983). Political Campaign Communication: Principles and Practices. New York: Praeger.

Weaver, D., and Drew, D. (1993). Voter learning in the 1990 off-year election: Did the media matter? Journalism Quarterly, 70, 356-368.

Weigold, M. F. (1991, May). Negative political advertising: Exploring mediating conditions of target and source effects. Paper presented at the annual meeting of the International Communication Association, Chicago.

Weigold, M. F. (1992). Negative political advertising: Individual differences in responses to issue versus image ads. In L. Reid (Ed.), Proceedings of the American Academy of Advertising.

Weigold, M. F. (1993, April). Effects of negative information: A review and summary from psychology and communications. Paper presented to the annual meeting of the Popular Culture Association, New Orleans.

West, D. M. (1993). Air Wars: Television Advertising in Election Campaigns, 1952-1992. Washington, DC: Congressional Quarterly Press.

West, D. M., Kern, M., & Alger, D. (1992, September). Political advertising and ad watches in the 1992 presidential nominating campaign. Paper presented at the annual meeting of the American Political Science Association, Chicago.

Westley, B. H. (1981). The controlled experiment. In G. H. Stempel III and B. H Westley (Eds.), Research Methods in Mass Communications, (pp. 196-216). Englewood Cliffs, NJ: Prentice-Hall.

Wicks, R. H., & Kern, M. (1993). Cautious optimism: A new proactive role for local television news departments in local election coverage. American Behavioral Scientist, 37, 262-271.

Williams, F. (1986). Reasoning with Statistics: How to Read Quantitative Research (3rd ed). New York: Holt, Reinehart and Winston.

Wolinsky, L. C., Sparks, J., Funk J., Rooney E., Lyon, G, & Sweet, L. (1991, January/February). Refereeing the TV campaign. Washington Journalism Review, pp. 22-28.

Wood, W., Kallgren, C., & Priesler R. (1985). Access to attitude relevant information in memory as a determinant of persuasion: The role of message attributes. Journal of Experimental Social Psychology, 21, 73-85.

Wright, P. L. (1974). Analyzing media affects on advertising responses. Public Opinion Quarterly, 38, 192-205.

Zhao, X., & Bleske, G. L. (1995). Measurement effects in comparing voter learning from television news and campaign advertisements. <u>Journalism and Mass Communication Quarterly</u>, <u>72</u>, 72-83.

BIOGRAPHICAL SKETCH

Jennifer D. Greer was born in Columbia, Missouri, on August 4, 1966, and was raised in a suburb of St. Louis. She received a bachelor's degree in journalism and a bachelor's degree in political science, both awarded summa cum laude, from the University of Missouri-Columbia in 1988. She earned a master's degree with honors in political science from the University of Kansas in Lawrence, Kansas, in 1992. Later that year, she began doctoral studies in mass communication at the University of Florida in Gainesville, Florida.

Greer worked as a business and financial reporter at The Kansas City Star from 1988 to 1991. She then worked four years as a free-lance reporter. Greer also worked part-time as a writer in the news and public affairs offices at the University of Kansas and the University of Florida. From 1994 through 1996, she was managing editor for Sun.ONE, an on-line commercial newspaper produced by the University of Florida's College of Journalism and Communications and The Gainesville Sun.

In 1996, Greer became an assistant professor of journalism in the Donald W. Reynolds School of Journalism at the University of Nevada-Reno. She may be reached at the school at (702) 784-6531, Mail Stop No. 310, Reno, Nevada 89557-0040. Greer, her husband, Richard LeComte, and their daughter, Rachel, currently live in Reno, Nevada.

I certify that I have read this study and that in may opinion it conforms to the acceptable standards of scholarly presentation and is fully adequate, in scope and quality, as a dissertation for the degree of Doctor of Philosophy.

Michael F. Weigold, Chair
Associate Professor of Journalism and
Communications

I certify that I have read this study and that in may opinion it conforms to the acceptable standards of scholarly presentation and is fully adequate, in scope and quality, as a dissertation for the degree of Doctor of Philosophy.

Mary Ann Ferguson
Professor of Journalism and
Communications

I certify that I have read this study and that in may opinion it conforms to the acceptable standards of scholarly presentation and is fully adequate, in scope and quality, as a dissertation for the degree of Doctor of Philosophy.

Marilyn Roberts
Assistant Professor of Journalism and
Communications

I certify that I have read this study and that in may opinion it conforms to the acceptable standards of scholarly presentation and is fully adequate, in scope and quality, as a dissertation for the degree of Doctor of Philosophy.

Alan G. Sawyer
Professor of Marketing

I certify that I have read this study and that in may opinion it conforms to the acceptable standards of scholarly presentation and is fully adequate, in scope and quality, as a dissertation for the degree of Doctor of Philosophy.

John W. Wright, II
Professor of Journalism and
Communications

This dissertation was submitted to the Graduate Faculty of the College of Journalism and Communications and to the Graduate School and was accepted as partial fulfillment of the requirements for the degree of Doctor of Philosophy.

August 1996

_____
Dean, College of Journalism and
Communications

_____
Dean, Graduate School

CPSIA information can be obtained
at www.ICGtesting.com
Printed in the USA
BVHW011022231219
567578BV00001B/5/P